MEMOIRS OF A SHANNOCK

Memoirs of a Shannock

May Ayers

Line drawings by the author

Dedication

This book is dedicated to my beloved husband and a caring father, Bill Ayers, postman and postman higher grade at Sheringham Post Office for just over twenty years. And to two 'Shannocks', Henry Willie and Mary Ann.

The Larks Press

Published by the Larks Press
Ordnance Farmhouse, Guist Bottom
Dereham, Norfolk NR20 5PF

Tel./Fax 01328 829207
E-mail: larkspress@talk21.com

Printed by the Lanceni Press, Garrood Drive, Fakenham

First printed 1995
Reprinted 2001

British Library Cataloguing-in-Publication Data
A catalogue record for this book is available from the
British Library

Cover photograph:
Whelk coppers, Beach Road, Sheringham, c. 1903
L. to R:. Old Woodhouse, unknown, Father aged 18, 'Lotion Tar' Bishop

ISBN 0 948400 33 1

Foreword

For many years I have been attracted to the small town of Sheringham, sitting on the edge of the North Norfolk coast.

It has produced a particular race of fishermen.

Many have, and still do, serve in the Lifeboat service. Their families, their history and their deeds should be recorded for future generations to know.

Now my friend, May Ayers has written about the hard but sometimes humorous lives of these local families. I am delighted to be associated with this book and I am sure it will be read and enjoyed as a true record of past life in Sheringham.

Jason Partner

Introduction

When I first penned these words, I little imagined that they might be published, neither could I consider myself as an Author. In 1969 my father fell in his cottage, and broke his thigh, he was then 84 years old, and my mother was brought to my home and care. During his time in the Norfolk and Norwich Hospital he was seriously ill; then transferred to the Fletcher Hospital at Cromer. Under the doctors, nurses and staff there he made a marvellous recovery. I provided him with exercise books, chiefly to help his convalescence and to encourage him to recount his memories of days at sea, and Sheringham's early days. Mother had to join in too! As the exercise books were written, they were put away for some time, then I began my writing.

What a great pleasure it was for me to recall those days of a select little town, a fishing community proud of its traditions, a gentler pace of life, a determined and independent personality, the varied colourful characters that fished from these shores. These were the people we saw every day.

I hope this book will bring back many happy memories of the Sheringham we knew, and a glimpse of the past for those who have come to live amongst us.

May Ayers

Acknowledgements

My gratitude goes especially to a good friend Mr Jason Partner (artist) of Aylsham, whose sincere encouragement, in the early days of my writing, certainly spurred me on. Also my thanks to Mr John Lown (Sheringham) who as a 'go-between' ably assisted in transferring the hand-written chapters to Aylsham, to Mrs Bernadette Wright (Norwich), for her generosity and kindness in typing the complete manuscript, my warm thanks to Mr Peter Brooks for his valued advice and assistance and to many friends who said 'Why don't you write it all down?' This I have attempted. A special word of thanks to all my family, for their interest, help and encouragement and to Mrs Susan Yaxley (Larks Press) for having confidence in my work.

Picture Credits

Line drawings are the work of the author.
Author and publishers are grateful to those listed below for permission to use their photographs.

Page 25 , 77 & 94	Mr R. Hedges
Page 42	National Maritime Museum, Greenwich.
Page 45 & 84	Mrs J. Swallow and Mrs P. Franklin

1. Early Days

Sheringham is today a prosperous seaside town, bounded on the north by the sea. Stretching away to the south, east and west, new houses and new estates have sprung up like mushrooms overnight, indicating we hope that there is plenty of new life for the future. It can hardly seem possible to people who didn't know the town as it used to be that it can have grown and developed so quickly, but only about sixty years ago, when I came out of school as a girl, the adjoining road, now Barford Road, was edged by allotments and fields. We used to play here, and went along the path and through a gate into Beeston Road. A scattering of houses in that part of the town was just beginning to be built and most of Common Lane was still a country lane with hedges and a stream.

Of course life was at a leisurely pace - horses and carts, not today's motor transport. The main part of Sheringham's shopping area was, in my younger days, the lower part of the town, around the Clock Tower and towards the sea; there were some shops in Station Road and some in Church Street, but one was able to purchase everything that was required in those few streets. Co-operative Street and Wyndham Street were two of the busiest, with every conceivable shop in them. As we lived in Cremer Street practically all our shopping was done there. At the corner of Co-operative Street and Cremer Street was a large Co-operative store which sold everything: coal, coke, paraffin and general stores, drapery, ladies' and gents' clothing, furniture, carpets, lino and there was a shoe and boot repairing department and a bakery. The large bakehouse on the opposite corner of the same road was much used by many householders who took advantage of the availability of the large ovens at all times to have meat, pies, and tarts, even Christmas dinners, cooked here for a penny an item.

In Co-op Street there were two fried fish shops at one time, run by Henry Bishop, a first class butcher, Mr C. Dennis (known as 'Joe Willie'), a dairy and a men's outfitters, two fresh fish shops and the local barber's shop where the men collected together on a Saturday night to exchange all the latest gossip - more important than the weekly haircut or shave. Near by was old Mr Tyce, the shoe repairer, and further down was a vegetable shop and a general hardward store run by A. I. Cooper, selling household materials as well as paraffin oil and candles.

A short cut through Weston Street led us into Wyndham Street, again with many shops and businesses, two lovely cake and pastry shops, Lambert's and Lusher's - the latter remains today, but Lambert's is long gone. These bakehouses too were willing to allow the ladies, especially in the summer months, to make use of their ovens to bake large trays of meat, rabbit or pies.

There was a fresh fish shop near to the Lobster Inn, run by Wildredge and Smith; at Christmas the whole of the outside of the shop would be hung with poultry and game. Further down, on the same side, was Hannah Piggott's fruit and vegetable shop, and in my young days next door was a small newspaper shop where one could buy Sunday newspapers. Carrying along on the same side was a builder and plumber, then two cottages, then 'Old Black Bob's' (Bishop's) fish shop. I don't think anyone has ever come up to him for cooking fish and chips. We would queue here for a 'tuppenny and one' or a 'pennyworth of chips'.

1

Across the road was Mrs Storey's little sweet shop; it is almost the same today, but is a cycle repair shop. How many hours we would gaze into her window, looking at the shallow trays of sweets on display, sherbert dabs, cut cavendish (a kind of chocolate tobacco), liquorice dabs, huge bullseyes - these we would suck and then take them out of our mouths to see what colours they had changed into. There were huge chocolate-covered humbugs at a penny each. We never had much to spend, a few farthings maybe, and most of these things to be had were less than a penny. This meant we could get at least four things and it would take us all morning to make up our minds.

Near by was another shop, a general ironmongers, and this employed several people. There was also a furniture store where auctions were held, a small dairy and a flourishing boot repairers. At the top of Wyndham Street, almost opposite the Lobster, was a most select shop with large plate glass windows, Madame Elaine's, displaying perhaps one elegant gown in the window and a large arrangement of flowers in a huge vase. Next door was the Mauvaine Tea Rooms, later to become Pedlar's Pack. We could buy the best home-made ice-cream from the little shop on the corner of High Street and Co-op Street (this was the 'Allies' kept by old Mr 'Downtide' West) or we could go to Church Street where 'Bussey' Hannah too made delicious ice-cream. Quite a number of shops in the High Street would remain open on a Saturday night till nine o'clock with their bright lights shining . For fruit and vegetables we had the choice of Billington's, Hastings' and Cooper's. Barney's sweet shop with its choice selection and assortment of sweets, chocolate and tobacco was eagerly visited.

During the week there would be various dealers around the town selling their wares. Some would bring paraffin lamps and all the necessary articles for lighting the cottages. Then there would be fishermen or hawkers of fish, cockles and mussels, ringing their bells and shouting such things as 'Longshore herring, twenty for a shilling!' Out would come the old women and young wives with their aprons on and a basin to collect the wares. One dealer, a Mrs Grout, with her husband, always brought us our farm butter. She dealt with all farm produce, rabbits and chickens included. Her cart would be loaded and she inevitably soon sold out. A rabbit with its skin cost sixpence.

'Longshore herring, twenty for a shilling!'

My mother always skinned her own rabbits and she carefully dried and treated the pelts to make a large lined bedcover - it was very handsome!

There were many Frenchmen coming to the doors, some with bicycles, carrying strings of onions on their shoulders. Then, of course, another interesting event to us youngsters was to see the pedlar with his knife-grinding machine. He would park this object somewhere handy, then collect knives, scissors and shears to sharpen. We used to stand around the whole time to watch the sparks fly.

When old Paddy the organ-grinder came, which was generally in the summer, he would patrol around the streets with a monkey on top of the organ. Sometimes, if we hung around long enough, he might allow one of us to turn the handle while he had a refresher in the nearest pub! Of course this was in the old days, not long after the First World War,and we would see several poor chaps, blind, crippled and legless, begging for money. One

Carrying strings of onions

of these came always in a wheel-chair; he had no legs and arrived each summer. He balanced a zither on his chair and played it beautifully - it was fascinating to watch him. We would follow him from street to street, just watching him play.

These days always seemed hot and sunny; most of the days would be spent on the beach and our mothers would have to come and drag us home. Hours we spent on the hot sand, playing childish games. The council water-cart would come through the town regularly and as it went along it sprayed all the dirt and dust away. On really hot days the steam would rise from the road as it went along and we kids would delight in running behind it.

One of the old Sheringham characters so popular with us was 'Old Go-Father Pegg'. He was a very enterprising fisherman and always wore a red trilby hat. He had a small boat which he would want to get up and down the beach, so he would entice us all to sing,

> 'Look upon the wall - you'll see a great spider,
> Glory to his great long legs.
> Wibbledy, wobbledy, hit him on the nobbledy,
> Then you'll see no more cobwebs.'

We would then heave his boat over the sand to low water, hoping we would be lucky enough to have a trip with him. We were often promised some 'cooshies' (local word for sweets) when we came ashore if we stayed to get his boat up again. Needless to say we *did* wait, all for a longed-for sweet. He would throw handfuls of 'cooshies' up in the air and a mad scramble for them would begin. I think the boys usually got the most!

Such was Sheringham when I was young, and I should like to write down a few things about those days gone by. Really I feel this is my father's story more than mine, so many times he has told me tales of Sheringham in his childhood. How often I have wished that I wrote it all down as he told me! He had a wonderful way of telling a yarn and a good memory too. His tales were fascinating about his days at sea and all the old Sheringham characters. Most of them have now passed on, but while they lived there was a wealth of knowledge to be gained from these old people who lived so close to the sea.

Those of us children who came from fishing families all knew how hard it was for our parents to make a decent living. Many had large families to support, but were undoubtedly better off than some of the labourers or other workers. Usually the children were fairly healthy, brought up on soups and stews nade from sixpennyworth of bones from the butcher's shop. The stewpan was always simmering away on top of the stove, with vegetables grown on the allotments and a rabbit or two, probably obtained by poaching.

A fishing life was hard, with not much to be caught. Maybe in the summer months, when crabs and lobsters were plentiful, they would live a little better, but winter months would bring hardship. My father would go to sea for whelks or codling, but there were not the high prices of today. Lots of times when he came ashore he couldn't sell his catch because there was no money about. Once he strung up several dabs and plaice on strings with the idea of going round the doors to sell them; he came back very disheartened - he had sold very few. These were the days when housewives found even cheap fish beyond their means. So the whole catch was put into wicker peds and he took them on his barrow to the National Children's Home in Sheringham.

Although my father went to sea, I could hardly ever persuade him to take me with him. One boat he had was the *Little May* and his partners were Jimmy 'Mace' Johnson and 'Dingy' Middleton. They went from the West End beach as he had two sheds on West Cliff. One was near by the *Henry Ramey* Lifeboat shed, where most of his gear was stored, and many hours I played here whilst he mended his pots and gear. Another was near the old whelk coppers. The boats would land there near the steps leading to the coppers and their catch would be carried up, washed, weighed and boiled.

Sometimes he would take me off to his crab-pots, warning me not to be seasick or he'd have to bring me ashore. On one of my earliest trips, when I was quite young, I must have looked rather green and he got another crab-boat returning to the beach to bring me home. Luckily I was never seasick and would remain in the boat, anchored off the beach, whilst he went home for a meal.

Most of my friends were from fishing families too and we lived near enough to each other to play around the old street lamps in the winter time, enjoying such games as 'Tip finger whip', a kind of catching game, guessing who had touched your finger whilst your back was turned. This was a great favourite - if one guessed correctly, that person would have to take your place. 'Warn you once' was another chasing game, where hands were linked up to catch the culprits who had been warned. Games of hopscotch were also chalked on the pavements. 'Hide and seek' would take us up and down the alleyways and into many old yards and corners.

Valentine night, February 14th, was one which the old Sheringham families held dear. There was much activity on this night when presents and small gifts were thrown in the doors. All children would find this quite exciting as various things wrapped in paper and tied to string would be thrown in and snatched back again. Often these were joke things like lumps of coal or an old scrubbing brush. We knew that it was our grandfathers or uncles who were playing these tricks upon us, but we did get oranges and sweets too. When we got old enough to play these tricks ourselves, we would collect together all sorts of things, dummy bars of chocolate, empty boxes wrapped up, all sorts of oddments, to take around and throw in through the doors. This was called 'Snatch Valentine' and usually meant running around the old alleyways and cottages near by.

Although we had this sort of fun, we never attempted to do anything that would bring the law down upon us or our families. If we were seen climbing the slopes from the promenade the beach inspector would be after us, and no one would have dared to have carved a name on the seats in the shelters, for this might mean court procedures. My parents always warned me to stay away from any person who had been involved with the police and of course we respected the wishes of our parents.

Guy Fawkes night was another time for our high spirits. When older we would usually collect together on the Furrow Common (Beeston Common). As soon as it was dark the boys would set alight all the gorse bushes; they blazed from end to end and we could smell the burning gorse long before we got near. Police would appear on the scene and boys would scatter in all directions. The thing I most enjoyed was the guy that my mother would have prepared by the time I got out of school. This was a large colourful mangel which would have a grinning face and a candle inside all ready to light when it was dark. Then I would go with some of my little friends - we were like so many hobgoblins - criss-crossing the road, in and out of gardens, knocking on doors, crying 'Penny for the guy!'.

Once a friend, Ellen, asked if she could go with me. It was a very rough night with squalls of wind and rain. We were in the High Street when suddenly the hat of her guy blew off. Ellen's guy was actually a turnip that her granny had scraped out for her. When the wind blew the lid of her guy away, all visions of any money she might have acquired speedily vanished. She began to cry, so away we went to see the granny in her cottage near the sea front. Now *my* mother always secured the lid of my guy with safety pins which kept the whole thing windproof and alight. This little scraped-out turnip which Ellen had, had lost its top and its light, but the old lady was far too engrossed in studying the horse-racing results in the daily paper to bother about a lid or hat for the guy. I shall never forget how comical it was when she picked up a large saucepan lid and put it on top of the turnip, saying, 'There yar - you kin go out with that - thass alright'.

Having very little pocket money, we were always doing things to bring us a few extras. As it neared Christmas time our thoughts would turn to carol-singing, probably starting as early as the first week in December, only to be scolded on the doorsteps and told to come back later. Our usual haunts were the large houses on Hooks Hill and Abbey Road where quite likely we would see other boys and girls doing the same thing. The word would soon go around who paid the most; generally our reward would be a penny. Sometimes we were asked to sing to the folks inside; I don't remember being too shy to do this - our ages were about ten or eleven years old. We went in small groups and sang as nicely as we could. I never remember us misbehaving; we were polite and closed the gates. Probably we would end up with five shillings or so and this would be put away to buy our sisters and brothers their Christmas presents. Quite a lot of us would make for Mr Stanley Christopherson's house; he was a philanthropist and a businessman who always gave good money - sometimes we got half-a-crown from him.

Once I remember we were out around the roads singing our carols - it was a beautiful moonlit night - when we met four or five boys and they informed us that a lady, Mrs Oaks, who lived in a bungalow on the Rise, had lost her little black scottie called Peggy and if we found it there was a reward of one pound. To us this was quite a fortune, so we hoped we should find Peggy. Just as we entered Cremer's Drift, there, going before us, was the little dog in question actually on its way home. We hurried after it, calling out its name. It turned and looked at us and then proceeded on its way. We weren't going to miss this opportunity, it was too good by half, so we kept up beside it and it calmly headed along to its garden and home. We tentatively also went in and knocked on the door. The door opened and a tall lady called out, 'Oh you darling girls, you've found my Peggy! You must come in, do come in - which one of you is the eldest? I must give you your reward.' The little dog, worn out with its wanderings, was only too eager to get into its basket near the fire, whereupon we were told we had to see her Peggy go to bed, we were such good girls, and a ten shilling note was given to me as the eldest for us to share. When we left the little house we knew that the boys would not be far away and they would be eager to get the money and maybe would be lying in wait. A small wooden fence and bushes surrounded the garden and, with our hearts beating with fear and anticipation of an ambush, we somehow hurtled ourselves out of the garden and sped along the road and down Common Lane to home and safety. I don't think our feet touched the ground and, on reaching home, my mother was able to change the note and the four of us had half-a-crown each.

Paddy the organ-grinder man might let us turn the handle
while he had his half pint.

2. Childhood

The Great War of 1914-18 had just another eighteen months to drag on when, on Tuesday May 15th 1917, Mother decided to shop. No doubt, like a bird, she was getting in stores ready for all eventualities. On feeling unwell, she quickly returned home, summoning the midwife, Mrs Eake, who conveniently lived only two doors away in Cremer Street. That afternoon, during a severe thunderstorm, I was born. Many years later Mother told me how she thought the house was struck by lightning and the same night the Zeppelins crossed the coast, dropping their bombs, with the sky illuminated with search lights.

I was the third child born to my parents, Mary Ann and Henry William West; their first daughter, Ena Elizabeth, was born some eight years before, and their only son, Henry Robert, followed two years later in 1910. My father, known as Henry 'Joyful' West, belonged to an old Sheringham fishing family; his father, grandfather and great-grandfather had made the sea their calling.

The little cottage in Cremer Street, Sheringham, consisted of two bedrooms, toilet and landing, and a large bright and sunny front room. One didn't call it a sitting room in those days - at least *we* didn't - it was always the front room and only used occasionally. Now and again a fire would be lit in its tiled hearth and the reflections of its flames would dance on the bright fender and tongs. A lovely mahogany side-board, Mother's pride and joy, stood on the south wall; the bay window contained two small chairs, with the inevitable aspidistra in its jardinière for all to see. In the corner the only musical instrument at that time was the well-used His Master's Voice gramophone. The large room held the dining table, set of chairs, two arm chairs and sofa, with the grandfather clock in the corner and large Edwardian prints on the walls, plus carpets and rugs. It was always a great pleasure to me when it was decked with holly and mistletoe and the meals taken in the comparative comfort of an open fire at Christmas time.

Adjoining this was the kitchen with its cheerful range; this was much more the living room and parlour, warm cosy and cheerful, in which Mother cooked, sewed, mended clothes, renovated and stitched on the old sewing machine, and we were washed here, either sitting on the kitchen table, or in the old tin bath brought in from the shed, in front of the fire. Above this was a rack where clothes were kept warm and aired for us to wear.

In the corner was the white-washed pantry; this could be entered by a door which led under the stairs. Here were shelves of crockery and china, with jars of preserves and other goods. It was quite large, and under the staircase was a wooden chest with a lid; this was the container for my father's shirts, ganseys, pants and boot stockings, ready for any time when he came home from sea and needed dry clothes. The scullery was used for washing and mangling linen; it was small with a window, under which was a table and another one opposite. The old copper in the corner, where the water was boiled, was replenished constantly with old bits of wood or the remnants from Father's crab-pots. He always kept a good supply of these in the shed at the bottom of the garden, and the furnace would gobble them up fast enough. The mangle which stood in the corner behind the door was a great asset and cost £6 from the Co-op! Linen was often pegged out in the passage-way between the houses; this was a good drying area in wet weather, but you had to don several layers of clothes when hanging them out in the depth of winter!

There was a regularity about the week's chores in those days; certain days called for the same procedure and hardly anything was allowed to interfere with the weekly routine. Monday was taken over entirely with the week's wash. The old copper in the corner of the scullery would be lit at first light, ready to begin boiling all the white linen. This had to be rinsed in the small square sink and finally 'blued' with the dolly-bag Reckitt's Blue, after which the coloureds were done, and last of all the boot stockings and ganseys. The whole day would be taken up with washing, mangling and hanging out, then scrubbing the floors and tables, cleaning out the fire, emptying the copper with a hand-cup and re-laying the fire for the next week's boil. Tuesday was given over to ironing, using the old cast-iron flats heated on the range, one at a time. Also the shopping had to be done. Wednesday meant baking for the family and a general clean through. Bedrooms were usually cleaned up and tidied by Thursday, with more shopping. Friday saw much activity for the weekend. It was the day in our house for the great clean, windows, brasses, chairs put outside with rugs, everything having a sweep down and a polish. My mother kept her kitchen range polished so one could see one's face in it; she always rose early for this, so it was always sparkling when we sat down to breakfast. The lino was washed and polished.

On Saturday Mother baked her pies and tarts, always two loaves of bread and most probably rabbit and pork for the weekend - the little kitchen range would be red hot with all the things she flung into it. In the summer that little room caught all the early morning sun and became like a hot-house, then all the doors and windows would be flung open. Then came Sunday, a day given over to rest and relaxing, with visits to church or chapel and often to our grandparents. It was a different atmosphere on a Sunday; everything that needed doing was done the night before: all shoes were cleaned, smart clothes were laid out ready for us to wear, we would have our baths before the kitchen fire, and my hair was curled up with pieces of linen rag tied up on my head; these were called 'Dodemans'. We were never allowed to buy sweets upon a Sunday, or play cards. If I knitted during that day my father would say, 'You can put that away, you've had all week to do that'. Mostly the day was spent in walks and visiting relatives.

We were lucky enough to have a happy and secure home although moneywas often scarce. We did not expect much from either of our parents; most families were in the same boat, and many families had a meagre existence. Our parents did all they could to ensure we had the necessities of life; we could not be indulged, but somehow we always had sufficient plain, but good, food and were brought up to respect our elders. My mother

...in the tub before the fire.

8

was very much concerned for our health - more than for our education. Of course we attended school regularly, but her main interest was to have us well and she called in the family doctor whenever we were ill. I had very indifferent health in my early life and had to be often away from school, making it hard for me to catch up with the other pupils.

Home remedies were used by the fishermen's wives. This was their cheapest resource and they had many standbys as they could not always afford to call the doctor. Regularly on a Saturday night, we were dosed with a spoonful of syrup of figs. When we looked wan and pale, out would come the Parish's Food, a good tonic, but it had to be taken through a straw to protect our teeth! Baked onion, hot and wrapped in a cloth, was placed on our ears for earache (which I got repeatedly); for toothache we might have oil of cloves or salt heated up and placed in a bag, which Mother had made, and held on the offending area. Throughout the winter time I wore a liberty bodice, a warm garment much used. Into this Mother would sew a small lump of camphor in a tiny bag; this was supposed to keep colds and coughs away - it didn't seem to do the trick with me, I got just as many! Also she possessed an old box which held some very old-fashioned long tallow candles used regularly for all sorts of complaints. The chief one I recall was when she cut heart shapes from brown paper and rubbed them all over with the tallow candles. These were then put next the skin on to our chests to prevent coughs. I think I got more than anyone else - they didn't stay in the place where they were supposed to and would often drop into the lower regions. One hardly dared move in case the offending article protruded from the bottom of a knicker-leg or something. When we got chilblains it was the accepted thing to dip our sore feet into the chamber pot containing the first water of the day. If we suffered toothache and the tooth was a bit loose, a cotton was tied around the tooth and then to a door handle. The child was sat in a chair, the door was slammed and the tooth out!

Mind you, the family doctor never failed us when we were ill. Old Doctor Sumpter came maybe two or three times a day, whether it was measles or mumps. Like most of the doctors of those days he was never sure of getting his money from the folks he attended; it

...*one of the large automobiles..*

was a problem for the poor to be able to pay, but he would say to Mother, 'Now Mary, you're not to worry about the money, you call me in.' She had great faith in him.

The doctor usually arrived in one of the large automobiles then coming into fashion, a huge thing with large lamps on the sides, always chauffeur-driven by Billy Bumfrey who would sit outside and wait for the doctor to emerge. Once he came when we all caught mumps, one after the other, and all lay side by side. About a week later, it being just before Christmas, Mother had bought us some coloured paper to make paper chains; we had been making these in bed and were ready to hang them up. We were proceeding to do so when he came suddenly in - we got a severe talking to for being out of bed.

Another time, when I was much older, I had just been attending the scholarship at school and was ill for about six weeks with gastritis and an ulcerated mouth. He came each day to paint the inside of my mouth and was much concerned that I should not sit for any more scholarships!

Dr Sumpter lived in a very large house with a vast garden near to the railway line. (This is now the Tyneside Club.) Many times I sat in his waiting room; it was quite awesome, but it was intriguing to look at the pictures on the walls. Displayed there were pictures of five elderly gentlemen representing the five senses. Most of the families around us led quite simple lives with very few luxuries. Several families with eight or nine children lived in tiny cottages with one living room and one bedroom with a small 'back-us'. They had only an outside toilet and this had to be shared with four or five families; they had no washing facilities and had to fetch their water from the local pump at Lusher's corner or the reservoir at the Town Clock. We were luckier than some as we had water laid on.

One of my earliest recollections was of my father, who had been fishing out of Grimsby, returning home. At that time several fishermen had gone to Lincolnshire as money was in better supply there. Father and his partners felt that this was an opportunity to support their families and have a better income. Many remained in Grimsby and their descendants are there to this day. I can remember Mother taking me along the promenade in a pushchair, seeing Father and his partners land on the shore, and an old tin box being handed ashore; when he came up the beach, it was to bring me a teddy bear. That teddy was my joy, but for some reason I did not want its ears on and promptly took them off. Mother would diligently sew them back on and I would take them off. I was about two and a half at that time - the episode remained with me for life.

Another early memory was before I started school, about the age of four. Each day my brother and sister had come home from school much concerned about a poor black cat which was being ill-treated in the school playground and had asked if they could bring it home. At this Mother was adamant and tried to console them both by saying it was probably owned by somebody and would find its way home again. A few days later - it had been a cold wintry day with squalls of snow and sleet and Mother had been busy at the wash-tub all day - I was playing with my toys before the kitchen fire when suddenly outside in the passage-way there was the sound of running feet. The back door was flung open and the poor bedraggled cat was thrown in. Terrified, it hid under the sofa, later to be coaxed out. For several days it needed nursing and would not come near us children, but, with patience and care, eventually the cat took to us and made its home - but it was forever having kittens. Mother didn't have the heart to turn it out, but she got so fed up with finding homes for all the young cats that she said, 'The cat will have to go - I can't put up with this no longer!' She said to Father, 'I'm going to take the cat out tonight and pop it over someone's garden wall - someone will take it in'. My dad just smiled. Anyway she took the cat inside her coat to keep it warm and I went with her, far too young to realise we might be losing puss. For some while she looked over all the garden fences, wondering who would be kind enough to keep the cat. We seemed to walk for ever, and at last she found what she thought would be a suitable home and left the cat there. Making haste for home, she didn't say a word. Back inside the warm kitchen, Father cast his eyes up and said nothing. With a tear or two she prepared some supper, but she needn't have shed them for, within a few minutes, Tibbles was back on the doorstep and made straight for hearth and comfort. So Tibbles became our cat, a permanent member of the household. She loved the fireside and, in her old age, would often get inside the oven when the door was leftopen. She hardly moved, even when hot coals fell from the grate. We often smelt singeing fur and would have to move her to safety.

When I was eight years old we acquired our first puppy. My brother had wanted one for a long time, but our parents felt, if a dog was installed in the house, they would have the bother of looking after it, so they kept saying he could have one when he was older. Anyway his wish was not granted and every so often the request for a dog would be made again. Sometimes Mother would be willing but Father would not, sometimes the other way round. Then they would compromise and say, 'If you have a dog, you've got to look after it'. Then one lovely sunny morning, it was a Sunday and Bob with his pals had been over the golf links. I went everywhere with him and his chums; he never seemed to mind although he was six years older than me. I loved going with them all, either fishing in Augyn Beck or camping in the woods, rather than going with my sister and her girl friends. As we were coming through the town we met one of his school chums named Ellis Pratt who was carrying a black spaniel puppy.

Touching the puppy, Bob said immediately, 'Wherever did you get that?', and was told it was one of a litter in a stable at the bottom of Waterbank Road. We set off at once to have a look at this spaniel and her puppies and there they were, all lying beside her. Bob stooped down and picked up the only one which was a lovely chocolate brown. We hurried home, hoping that Mother would allow us to keep it. At the first sight of the puppy she fell in love with it and said we could keep it if it wasn't too much money. The bitch actually belonged to Mr Cutty West, a cousin of Mother's, and fortunately for us he only charged 10/-. Thus we were able to keep 'Nigger', a family pet much loved by us all, but he was Mother's devoted slave. He would never go for a walk without carrying her gloves or something that belonged to her. Usually on a Sunday evening Father and I would take a walk over the golf links and Mother would go to chapel. When she came out, she would come to meet us and the dog would be the first to spot her from the top of Skelding Hill; he would hurtle his body towards the figure he could see approaching as she came through the gate near the Grand Hotel. He lived until he was nine years old; we all mourned his passing and said we would have no more dogs, but eventually we did, and 'Prince' was my dog, but that's another story!

Mother and Nigger, about 1927

In those days when I was very young, I seemed to go everywhere with my brother. He never grumbled or complained at having me, whereas my sister Ena, who was eight years older, would trail me along with reluctance, especially if the current boy friend was waiting, making the remark to her friends, 'I've got to have *her* today'.

One Sunday morning quite a gathering of us went to Upper Sheringham looking for primroses. There were at least eight of varying ages, me the youngest, about four years old, the others much older. Some of us were dressed in our Sunday best and were carrying little baskets which had held our Easter eggs. Amongst the assortment of children were my brother and sister, some of the 'Lobster' Farrows and a couple of cousins. I don't remember walking there or the journey back home; my most vivid recollection was of being chased across a large ploughed field, my poor little legs not long enough to stretch across each furrow, clutching my basket of primroses, and of girls and boys flying in all directions to get away from the irate gamekeeper. He eventually caught us up and gave us a good talking to, taking away all of our primroses plus each small basket. Evidently we were on private land owned by the Upcher family. When we reached home and told our parents, my mother was furious; she was determined to go to Upper Sheringham to demand the baskets back, saying the game-keeper had no business to keep the children's baskets.

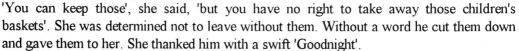

The old gamekeeper and his wife lived in a cottage in the Jericho Road leading out of Upper Sheringham village towards the heath. Mother knocked on his door When this was opened, in the mellow light of an old oil lamp she saw all the little baskets strung to the ceiling. The old man wanted to know what she wanted and she quickly told him. His reply was that the children were trespassing. His kindly wife who sat in the corner and could just be observed by the light from the fire, quickly admonished him saying, 'Oh John, you are a wicked old man to have robbed those poor little children'. Mother stood firm and told him she hadn't come for the primroses, 'You can keep those', she said, 'but you have no right to take away those children's baskets'. She was determined not to leave without them. Without a word he cut them down and gave them to her. She thanked him with a swift 'Goodnight'.

Ena, aged 12, Bob aged 9 and May, aged 2 and a half.

Not too long after this episode, again with Bob and his chums, we were all at the very end of the golf links - this seemed to be their favourite stamping ground. On this occasion we were in the lane leading over the railway line on to Weybourne Road near the Great Wood. Probably we were searching for birds' nests. Again I do not recall anything before or after the event; all I remember is finding my shoelaces undone and my brother tying them up for me when we heard an angry shout. Once more it was the gamekeeper and evidently we were trespassing again. He chased us as fast as he could, boys running in all directions. All could run faster than me, and my long-suffering brother was left behind to haul me along as fast as he could. In our haste my shoes had come undone and tears were flowing. Clutching my hand, Bob said, 'For Gawd's sake leave off blaring, we'll be alright'.

3. School Days

My first beginnings at Sunday school were at the Salvation Army Citadel, not many paces away from my home in Cremer Street; no doubt Mother thought it was near and handy. Our morning or afternoon classes were held in the little hall at the back of the building. Quite a lot of my little friends attended and they were jolly occasions when we sang,

> 'Jesus wants me for a sunbeam, to shine the whole day through.'

and

> 'Jesus bids us shine with a clear pure light,
> Like a little candle burning in the night.'

Old Mary 'Rufus' West was one of the teachers, and we would have our books marked with a star. One of the earliest treats I remember going to as a tiny child was to Morley Hill, accompanied by my sister, Ena; we were taken on wagons. There were many of us and it seemed wonderful as we streamed on to the large grassy hill where everything was set out for our enjoyment. In my young mind this was indeed the 'Green hill far away, without a city wall' about which we sang lustily in Sunday school, and quite expected to see the Cross on high.

I enjoyed my early days at the Army; it was bright and cheerful and we would have magic lantern shows (paying a penny, old money), Christmas teas and parties. When we acquired our first puppy, Nigger, I wanted to stay at home and look after him, but the Army officer came knocking at the door, wondering why I hadn't attended the Sunday school that day. 'Come along,' he said, 'the little dog will be alright till you get home.' Reluctantly I went with him, but all was well. Now at this time my sister and brother were going to the United Methodist or 'Bottom chapel'. This cosy little chapel in Beeston Road adjoined our garden and we were able to climb the grassy bank to reach the little graveyard which was there. There were about fourteen graves with their head-stones on the south side of the chapel, some of the Olley family, Emerys and a prominent family called Barcham who played a big part in the chapel in early days.

Sheringham was well provided with places of worship. In Station Road there was quite a large building on the corner of New Road and opposite the Robin Hood public house; it had a grassed area surrounded by a low wall with iron railings. The Primitive Methodist chapel was known locally as the 'Top chapel', whilst the one in Beeston Road was the 'Bottom' one, regularly attended by most of the fishing families. Mother was devoted to this one and went twice on Sundays (she was in the choir) whilst Father preferred the one in Station Road, as his parents did. Another place of worship used by the fishing families was the chapel of ease on West Cliff; sadly two of these chapels have disappeared and flats and shops have come in their place.

Before long I joined my brother and sister at the Bottom chapel where our Sunday school class was held in the small room at the rear. We always looked forward to the treats as this meant a day in the country, taken on wagons drawn by horses. One of the very earliest I recall was going on a lovely sunny day to Felbrigg Hall. Quite a large crowd was in the cart and I was in the rear with my aunt. Several wagons had arrived in the grassed area enclosed by a wall and the horses were getting restless as some children were getting off. Suddenly the horse of the wagon that I was in shied, rearing up and almost upsetting the cart. Most of the children were off and only I was left, but fortunately someone in the crowd saw the danger and snatched me off.

For a number of years we went to the same place, Felbrigg, then the news went round that the other chapels were going much further than we were. They were going to Thurgarton Hall. It certainly sounded better, as all our friends confirmed, so we had to get our parents to agree to this. Today's youth would smile at our treats as they adventure far and wide, but we were thrilled as our wagons and carts, all drawn by horses, took us off to Thurgarton Hall. As we went along the air was full of the sweet scent of honeysuckle, with wild roses in the hedges and our young voices singing lustily.

Arriving at the Hall, we had the full use of the park to run races and play games which were organised for us. The sun always seemed to be shining and large trays of strawberries would be brought out from the Hall with urns of tea and jugs of lemonade. Lying around in the summer grasses and flowers was our idea of bliss. Evening shadows and a crescent moon would find us all tired out, returning home through the lanes with horses and wagons, singing our songs, the treat over for another year.

A great highlight of the Sunday school year was our Anniversary weekend, held annually when the warm weather arrived. Weeks of preparation went into this weekend event, everyone practising songs and recitations for the great day. For weeks they would be learning their 'pieces'. I tried to avoid this if I could as I was far too nervous to get up and recite; some could be quite lengthy and all participants would proudly present themselves on the platform, dressed appropriately for the grand occasion. My mother spent many hours preparing pretty dresses for me to wear; sometimes she would make three if she could afford it. One would be worn in the morning, another in the afternoon, and a special one for the evening performance. Most of the children who took part looked lovely in their flowered muslin or sprigged cotton dresses with pretty little straw hats, mostly trimmed with flowers, and all were very proud when their turn came to recite or sing whilst parents and grandparents looked on. The event would be spread over the whole weekend, culminating in recitations, hymn-singing and choirs.

At the age of fourteen, I joined some of my friends who were members of St Peter's church. We became much involved with various church activities and joined the King's Messengers, run by the Miss Sheringhams who lived in Avenue South.

Every Sunday, Mother would attend chapel. As soon as she left the cottage Father would decide to make home-made toffee for us or roast chestnuts. This was good fun as he would allow us to hold the cooling toffee in our buttered palms and pull, stretch and twist the toffee until it was like spun gold. Then we left it to get cold, finishing off with filling the toffee tin.

Ena and Bob were both very good at sketching and painting and they would take this opportunity to do exquisite black and white drawings. They were able to go to a class held at the school in the evenings and I looked forward to doing the same. Mother tried to get us drawing books and materials for Christmas. When she came back from chapel she would admire their work and, although I was six or eight years younger than them, I tried hard to achieve the same standard. Needless to say it was difficult, but I was determined to get her praise. She was never lavish with this, but it was this experience and the encouragement of my mother that gave me my love of painting.

As Ena and Bob became older, they took to inviting some friends in. Sundays were kept very religiously in most of the fishing families and card-playing was frowned upon. However, on some evenings when Father had gone down to 'look at the sea' and Mother to chapel, they would wind up the old gramophone and turn back the matting and rugs to dance. Things would go well till they heard the approaching footsteps of our parents, then they would hurriedly turn off the gramophone and roll back the carpet to restore some semblance of a well-behaved family!

Our grandparents, my father's family in Beeston Road, whom we called 'Granny and Grandad Joyful', were very strong methodists and would never have dreamt of doing anything on a Sunday. Everything was done on the Saturday night. all shoes cleaned and clothes got ready, and our sweets bought at the various shops that were open quite late on Saturday nights. Some families were so rigid as not to cook or wash up the dishes on a Sunday. We were expected to go to chapel two or three times a day and most often we went to see our grandparents. I would go with my father, sitting on the horse-hair sofa in some discomfort whilst they exchanged the news.

Living in Cremer Street was an advantage as I did not have far to go to my week-day school which was at the south end of Cremer Street and corner of Barford Road. It had been built in 1906, a large and airy school covering a considerable area, with class-rooms for the boys and similar ones for the girls and infants. When I heard the first bell on a Monday morning calling us to lessons, my stomach would sink into my boots and it was often with a reluctant heart that I went into assembly as the second bell went.

The infants' department was separate from the older children and had large class-rooms, assembly hall and outside toilets across the palyground. In the early years infants, boys and girls together, started between three and five years old and were accommodated in the section nearest to Cremer Street. There were three teachers here, Miss McGregor, Miss Poley and the head of this department, a Mrs Tansley, who was very strict and many pupils were in awe of her. I started school when I was five, Mother taking me on the first day. I was placed first in Miss McGregor's class and then with Miss Poley, who was a gentle, kind person - everyone loved her. We would assemble in the main hall, sitting on the floor, where we would learn simple sums and words and how to tell the time. Afternoons we all had to lie on truckle beds and try to go to sleep; this for me was most difficult. Some probably managed it, but I didn't, even when our fold-up beds were taken outside on a sunny day.

The school had a large playground with outside toilets for the older pupils, a shelter at the lower end and one at the top - these were later turned into class-rooms as the town grew. When we were seven years old we transferred to the upper department and girls and boys were separated. A tall wall stood between the two main playgrounds. In this was a large wooden door painted green; this was the dividing line between the sexes. It held a certain fascination for us, and if it was left ajar (which was seldom) girls and boys would peer through at each other. This was frowned upon by the teachers and we were all threatened with punishment. Most of us obeyed the rules, but there was great consternation when some girls ventured to put notes under the door for the boys. Many questions were asked until the culprits were found, resulting in most of them getting the cane. We knew when this happened as we saw them on the way to and from their punishment, leaving with tears.

Mr Day was the headmaster in the boys department in my day. Only once do I remember an occasion when girls and boys did lessons together, and that was when we sat for the scholarship. We were paraded into the boys' department, sitting in separate desks, looking at each other as if we came from another planet!

Our headmistress was Miss Call, loved and respected, a splendid teacher. Her sudden death came as a shock when it was announced, but fortunately she was followed by another excellent head, Miss Hall, who took great interest in her pupils. We had the usual mixture of teachers, some feared, some loved. Punishments were dealt out for lying, stealing and rudeness - usually the cane, quite a deterrent to most of us. One teacher, a Miss Black, was well liked but too lenient. She was often at the mercy of some of us who liked a joke. She took the cookery and housewifery course in a separate building from the main school. One day we were making pancakes with only enough ingredients to make one each. Then we were shown how to toss them. Of course someone had to toss hers so high that it hit the ceiling, bounced off and slid down the wall where it disappeared behind a very large kitchen cupboard. Months later, it was a day for cleaning all utilities cooking range, cupboards and equipment. As we got to the large wooden cupboard Miss Black said, 'Girls this has got to come out. You can't get all the dirt out like that!' Whereupon the object was moved and behold, there lay the pancake with several grey-looking lumps of dough amongst the spiders' webs and fluff. Miss Black looked at the mess, an expression of amazement on her face. Glancing at us all, she said, 'I wonder how long it has been since this cupboard was moved!'

Usually I went home for my dinner, but in the summer time Mother would pack me some sandwiches and a bottle of 'pop' so that, with the others, I could enjoy the beach. The trouble with this was that we would be so engrossed in games that all of us would forget the time and several mothers would gather on the beach to collect the truants.

Each class-room held a blazing fire surrounded by a large guard, most welcoming on winter days. These were also in the corridors, so in all there must have been 20 or 25 fires to light and clean out every day of winter.(These fires were attended to by a Mrs Bayfield who lived close by on Barford Road; her husband had died during the First World War.) Those of us who sat at the back of the class didn't receive much warmth, especially if some teachers stood with their backs to it all day!

We were visited regularly by the school dentist. When he arrived at the school he used a caravan-type of vehicle with a small flight of wooden steps leading up to

... a large white handkerchief to her mouth.

16

the entrance; it was here we had to sit for our examinations in the large dentist's chair. The dentist was a Mr Sumpter, brother to the family doctor we knew so well. Whenever he examined us, he had the inevitable cigarette hanging from his mouth, and the long grey ash would be perilously close to dropping into our open mouths! After the examination we would emerge thankfully from the caravan, clutching in our hands a piece of paper with the dreaded instructions for what was to be done. We took these home in the the vague hope that they would overlook them - not so, there was no escape.

A few weeks later, the dentist's van would arrive again for the dental work to be done. This surgery on wheels was always parked on an area opposite the school at the far end of the Council's depot yard, and in twos and threes we would wend our way to this, some sitting in a small cubicle whilst the patient had treatment, eventually coming out with a large white handkerchief to his or her mouth.

Another regular visitor was the doctor. We would partly undress and he would turn us around, exclaiming if we were thin or under-nourished. After one visit he recommended Virol to my mother; this couldn't have been easy to provide as money was short, but I took it regularly. We also had our sight tested and I remember him saying I had excellent eyesight. Then came the nurse - quite often. None of us cared for this very much. One by one we would visit her in the headmistress's room where we knelt down and placed our heads in her aproned lap while she looked for nits and lice. What humiliation! Everybody fared the same and,

young as we were, we felt a certain unease. Most of us had caring and very clean mothers, but of course there were the odd few who didn't. Another item which looked appalling was the purple ointment dished out for impetigo.

Sheringham Elementary school was indeed a very good school, our teachers taking a fair interest in all of us, but indifferent health kept me away from school for weeks at a time. I loved painting and received substantial help with this subject. In fact, loking back at it now, I realise how fortunate we were. We used pastels, coloured paper and watercolours; often a few flowers would be placed for us to sketch and paint and sometimes one of the girls would be a model and we would have to draw and paint hands, legs, feet and various parts of the clothed body. Our teachers showed us how to model form in watercolour and how to 'lift out' passages with brush and rag, excellent tuition which has served me well. Other lessons to enjoy were geography, nature, English and composition. Once a week we had debates, much enjoyed as some of us acted as chairmen.

Today's children are taken to far-flung lands by their schools; only once do I remember being taken out - on a nature walk through the woods. What a lovely surprise that was! Once a week we would go to the Recreation Ground on the Upper Sheringham Road to play netball, rounders and other games, marching in file there and back. The ground was used a lot by both boys and girls and sports days and competitions took place once or twice a year. One most important day was Empire Day when everyone participated in races of various kinds, parents coming along if they could. Teas and cakes were available with ginger 'pop' in the pavilion, the day culminating in the presentation of our Empire medals. 'Land of Hope and Glory' would be sung and we would march around the whole

'Rec' singing lustily. Proudly we would parade beneath the Union Jack blowing in the breeze to receive our medals from some very important person.

During playtimes we were supervised by teachers. All manner of games were played, marbles, five-stones, tossing cigarette cards, hopscotch. Games such as 'Tip finger whip' and 'Warn you once' I have already described, but there was also 'Sheep, sheep, come home', a great success with the young ones. A long line of children would line up against the wall ready to make a dash across to the other side without getting caught by the so-called 'Wolf'. One person would stand in the middle of the playground shouting out a warning and saying,

> 'Sheep, sheep come home, the wolf has gone to Devonshire,
> He won't be home for seven year, sheep , sheep come home.'

The 'Wolf' would be hiding somewhere and as the children made a wild dash across to safety, the Wolf appeared, springing out to catch one who would have to be the 'Wolf' for the next game.

The streets were our playground.

How strange it was that there was a certain time for various games. Suddenly everyone would acquire tops and whips and we would spend hours making them fly, chalking the tops with colours. Then we would pester the blacksmith to put a 'toe' in the top so it would spin faster. The next thing would be bowling hoops along the streets - old pram wheels, bicycle wheels, anything likely to roll would do. After this, out would come Mother's clothes line for our skipping games. Most of these games were also enjoyed under the street lamps after the lamplighter had come along at dusk, lighting the gas lamps with his long-handled implement. You must remember there were few cars then, only horses and carts-the streets were our playground.

In those far off days anyone who had the misfortune to be ill with an infectious disease such as scarlet fever had to be isolated for six weeks, and this meant going to Roughton Isolation Hospital for our area, so of course we dreaded getting anything like this. But if we got measles or whooping cough, the bedroom in which the child lay was out of bounds to the rest of the family and often attended by an aunt or relative. A sheet immersed in some mild disinfectant would be hung at the door of the room.

One memory, for me still quite vivid, was when my friend Margaret Bradley caught scarlet fever. It was at the height of summer, just as the school holidays were beginning. We had all contracted measles together, my close friends Bronnie, Margaret and I who were almost inseparable. We spent long hours together on the beach, playing and swimming. Margaret lived very near the sea, overlooking the beach, so this was convenient for changing our swimsuits and shoes. We were getting over the measles and had the coming delight of six weeks to enjoy when we were told by her aunt that Margaret had scarlet fever and was in the Isolation Hospital. Our spirits sank; we knew we would miss her and six weeks seemed a very long time. And so it proved, but naturally we enjoyed ourselves with other playmates on the beaches.

Then the day came for us to be back in school; summer holidays were over for another year. We returned a bit sadly to school. It was the first morning back and Margaret not yet out of hospital. About an hour after the commencement of lessons I was suddenly asked to come to the front of the class by Mrs Rollins. Rather apprehensive, I went forward and stood near her desk. What had I done? What was wrong? Nervously I stood waiting for her next words.

'May', she said, 'I think you have been playing with Margaret Bradley, Haven't you?'

'Yes', was my reply, hesitantly, still wondering.

'You must go home', she said 'you will probably get scarlet fever, so you must stay at home for three weeks. Get your coat and tell your mother.' I looked round at all the girls, who were staring at me, and went out.

The door of the class-room was adjacent to the lobby where all the coats hung. As I reached for my belongings, another class-room door opened and a girl appeared - it was my friend Bronnie. As she took her coat from the peg, she saw me and said, 'What are you doing?'

I replied 'I've got to go home because I might get scarlet fever because I played with Margaret.' She looked a bit shocked.

'Coo, so have I. I've got to go home too. I might get scarlet fever.' For a few seconds we exchanged glances, hardly believing our good fortune. Then it dawned on us - three whole weeks! We raced down the playground, out of the gate and home to break the news ... our mothers did not look on it with such delight!

Mother was busy amongst the soap-suds - it was washday and everywhere was full of steam. 'What are you home for?' she queried. I told her, Bronnie's mother the same. They viewed it with a different eye. Holiday-makers had departed, so we had the sea and sand to ourselves; the rock pools were our domain. Needless to say we never developed scarlet fever, and what gratification it was to answer the many queries from other children, 'Why aren't you at school?' with the reply, 'You can tell the teacher all you like, she *does* know about it.'

4. A Fisherman's Life

In those far off days there always seemed to be ships running ashore in a fog or a storm. There were not the mechanical aids which today's technology has produced. Being connected with the sea, its hazards were an accepted fact of life. We little thought maybe, of the dangers our fathers and brothers undertook as they sought to earn a living. All we were conscious of was that most of us were in the same situation. There were at least fifty more boats working from the beaches, and well over a hundred fishermen - in fact about half the population went to sea or were connected with it in some way. One's life was controlled by the sea. Meals were not as regularly timed perhaps as in households where the breadwinner had set hours. Although the younger members of a family took their meals at the regular times, often food was kept hot or switched around to fit in with sudden changes in weather conditions so that boats could get off to earn the daily bread. A fisherman's wife had to be prepared for all eventualities, her man perhaps getting up at unearthly hours such as two or three o'clock, having his breakfast then and home again with the tide, eating another hearty meal and off again to moor his catch and get it to the merchant or train, whichever the case might be. Not only this, but her day could never be planned. My mother was always a very patient woman. I rarely heard her grumble or complain when the food dried up in the oven, waiting for the boats to come in. Sometimes Father would come in unexpectedly and say, 'I'll have my dinner now. The weather's a bt better now we're going to try to get off.' Or she might just have his and my brother's meal ready to serve when he would surprise her by saying, 'Can't stop for that now, we'll have to

..clothes were soaking wet and had to be dried before the fire.

eat it later'. What with that and the heavy washing, I think I resolved then not to marry a fisherman, not to suffer the anxious nights and days, the oft-repeated loss of gear and nets in storms just as they had set their crabpots, and the uncertainties of the future.

The fishermen wore heavy clothing, long boot stockings hand-knitted by wives, slops of tan or blue worn over their hand-knitted 'ganseys' (Guernsey jumpers), big yellow oilskins, sou'westers and long thigh boots. Often these would be soaking wet when they had been in rough seas, and they would have to be dried out before the kitchen range. As I got older, I felt the kitchen didn't look as smart as it could and would remove some, but found they were always put back by Mother. She knew it was more essential to have her men cared for than any so-called smartness. The rack above the fire would hold their ganseys, shirts, stockings and vests ready for immediate use. Mother made all the shirts required from warm winceyette material; they had no collars. She also made flannelette vests and knitted the long drawers or underpants. She constantly knitted the boot stockings from 'hob' which she bought from 'Dowsey' Little's; most of the wives made the ganseys with their special patterns and would repair the sleeves and necks of them as they frayed and wore. Mother also made Father's slops. She would obtain the bleached calico and sew these up on her machine. Then they were 'tanned' in the copper with what I believe they called 'ponika'. Later when slops and shirts became obtainable in the shops, these were bought. On wash day, these things were kept until last as they contained so much salt. Quite a few of the houses had wash-houses attached and you could hang a lot of clothes in there. We did not possess one, so all the washing was done indoors in the small scullery and it was a whole day's business to complete this.

On a winter's night Father would bring in his crab-pots to mend and braid for the coming season. It was no good complaining about it, after all it was our bread and butter. Mother never stopped him doing this although she was meticulously clean in the home; she knew better than to tell him to braid elsewhere. He was never the tidiest of persons and certainly believed that his home was his castle. He was quite content in the warm kitchen in front of a blazing fire on which he would casually throw some of the old crab-pot net and the flames would rise, sometimes nearly setting the chimney alight.

Mother would be at the table, either sewing his shirts, mending or knitting. Father would lay lines for codling. This meant baiting up the lines with mussels. He would bring the pack of lines into the scullery and bait up. I hated this, couldn't bear the scraping of his 'shut-knife' on the shell, and was very glad when he acquired a shed at the end of the garden and could go in there. With the aid of a candle or an old paraffin lamp, he could manage quite well. Later on, my brother built a very large concrete-block shed where they could store crab-pots, nets and gear, and Bob decided it would be sensible to build a chimney and install a small stove. Not only would this be ideal for their work, it would give more comfort indoors. Before this could be done, Father bought a second-hand oil stove and decided to try it out in the shed. The shed had a window and a door at the far end. One very windy day, he went into the shed with his pots to mend and we got on with our work indoors, glad to have time to ourselves to get various cleaning jobs done. As it neared dinner time, Mother remarked, 'Father has been there all morning - I wonder if he's alright. He hasn't come indoors for his cup of cocoa all that time - anyway he'll have his dinner now'. As we dished up the dinner he came up the yard and into the kitchen. At first we didn't notice, but when we looked at him again, he was like a nigger minstrel except for his eyelids which were pale in comparison. He was quite black and cobwebs of soot were all over him, even his moustache! He didn't take to our rolling about with laughter. When he looked in the mirror he said, 'I thought that seemed a bit funny. When I looked out of the window I thought it was foggy.' The whole of the shed was festooned inside with soot from the oil stove. It didn't take Father long to get rid of that and put in a proper stove.

My father had started his life at sea as a very young man with his father, Joshua Henry West, so he had learnt a great deal from him and his forbears as they were all fishermen for at least six generations. I can remember the early days when he was partners with Fred 'Dingy' Middleton and Jimmy 'Mace' Johnson and the boat they went in was the *Little May* and fished from the West End gangway. Later on when Bob was old enough to go to sea, he went with Father for many years and they got along very well together.

Crew of the Little May: L to R Jack Craske, Jim 'Mace' Johnson, Father and Fred 'Dimgy' Middleton

In those days the living was hard. The boats were rowed by hand and they had large tanned sails. Later, of course, engines were put into the boats which made their lives a bit easier, but as many did not have sufficient money to install their own engines, they had to resort to engines being put in by a merchant. Their catch had to go to him and they were obliged to accept the price that was offered, often a meagre amount. They were tied boats and not able to obtain higher prices elsewhere. They worked three or four men to a boat and boats, gear, crab-pots and buoys all had to be maintained. They braided and mended their pots with manila twine before the advent of nylon. During the winter, when the weather was bad and they couldn't get off after cod or whelks, they would prepare pots for setting in early spring, often to have them lost or smashed to pieces in the storms and gales which often occurred then. Many would lose gear worth hundreds of pounds and start the year off in debt. Quite a number of boats did get off to the whelk grounds during the winter, two miles back of the sands, which would be six or seven miles off the coast. They would come ashore near the steps that led up to the old whelk coppers and the bags of whelks were carried up to be washed and boiled ready for the market. Later on, these premises were bought and a large house was built and owned by a Mr Myerstein and called the Whelk Coppers. He took a great interest in the fishermen and had witnessed the hard work they had in hauling up their boats by hand-winch, so he installed the first electrical winch on the West End gangway for their use and later one for the East Beach.

Many of my friends were the daughters and grand-daughters of fishermen and lifeboatmen, so we were often alarmed when the lifeboat had to go off to the fishing boats. In bad weather storms can spring up quickly along the North Norfolk coast. Boats can launch in a calm sea, but winds can quickly change the sea into a dangerous aspect and the whelk boats will have to leave their pots and race for home. It is this sudden deterioration in weather that has taken so many lives along this coast when boats are trying to reach the shore through the breakers. It was on one such occasion, February 17th 1931, when Jack Craske was lost. The day had been fairly fine to begin with when about seven whelk boats went out, but by 2.30p.m. the weather had become very bad, with snow squalls and strong winds. It was one of the earliest tragedies I recall and made a lasting impression on our lives. I was at school at the time, with other friends whose fathers and brothers were at sea, when we heard the maroons fired about three o'clock. Although alarmed, there was nothing we could do until the final bell went for our release - it seemed an age before we could go. When I reached home it was to find an empty house, hot food still on the range and dishes scattered on the table. My first thought was 'Is Father alright? And the others, how are they?' Running down Beach Road, I met others bent on the same mission; a few were returning home and they told us the story.

As the weather had worsened, with snow squalls raging, those on shore considered the lifeboat should be launched, so the *Henry Ramey* was quickly pulled down the gangway. All the boats had returned safely except two, *Welcome Home* and *White Heather*. In the *Welcome Home* were Jack Craske, 'Pinny' Little and 'Sparrow' Hardingham; their boat capsized as it was coming through the breakers some 50 yards from the beach and her crew were thrown into the surf. The Cromer lifeboat, now on the scene, got alongside the men and Jack was pulled aboard and taken back to Cromer in a serious condition. The *White Heather,* manned by Jim 'Paris' West and Bob 'Rally' West, was having trouble in the breakers. The lifeboat crew had thrown life-jackets to several and, pulling Jimmy and his partner aboard, proceeded to tow the boat in. But this was swamped and gradually disappeared to become a total wreck further along the beach when it was finally washed ashore. Meanwhile Jack Craske was being taken to Cromer Hospital, but he never regained consciousness.

I remember the feeling of great sadness which prevailed in the town at the loss of such a fine young man who had left a young wife and two small children. Being a small fishing town, with most families related to one another, when these tragedies occurred it affected the whole town. On the day of Jack's funeral at the little chapel in Beeston Road, crowds of people lined the road and filled the chapel. Ironically it was a lovely spring-like day, calm and peaceful in contrast to the storm which had taken his life.

We were always quick on the scene if a ship came ashore, which was often the case. Sometimes it would break up or become a wreck in a very favourable position near a gap in the cliffs. This was a great advantage to anyone in the vicinity if they were laden with coal or wood. Folks would be seen going backwards and forwards with carts, prams and bikes, trying to get the spoils. One such was the *Gold Crown* - she ended up near East Runton Gap. Every conceivable means of transport was negotiating the narrow lane and going right into her hold, loading up carts, barrows and sacks before the coastguard got there to stop them. Bikes were being wheeled along the beach from all directions in order not to miss out on getting some of the cargo.

One of the very first ships to come ashore that I can remember was the *Ingeborg* from Helsingborg - I think this was 15th November, 1925. She was a four-masted schooner and ran ashore, high and dry, at Spaller Gap near Weybourne. Crowds of people trudged over the far end of the golf links to witness this sight. Mother took me, but also pushed an old wooden pushchair, no doubt for me if I got tired. I clearly remember going down on to the beach and walking all around the ship with my brother. The skipper seemed none too pleased and was pacing the deck with a large black dog. He was extremely agitated and at first refused to have anything to do with the boats or lifeboat which had turned up. Crowds of people had assembled on the cliff edge to await the outcome. The sea was quite calm. Two tugs arrived from Great Yarmouth, the *George Jewson* and the *Yare*. High tide was expected at six o'clock and it was said by everyone that 'If she doesn't get off then, she won't'. Most of us returned about half past five to see the effect of the tugs who had her in tow. My father and his mates in the *Little May* with *Sunbeam* and *Welcome Home* had been asked to assist the *J. C. Madge* which was to accompany the tugs to Yarmouth. Just on six o'clock, when the tide was full, we could see the tugs straining to refloat her. Suddenly she began to move and we watched her sail away. Later there was a lot of dispute between the owners and lifeboat crew plus boat-owners regarding some salvage money.

High and dry, the four-masted barque, Ingeborg from Helsingborg,
at Spaller Gap c. 1927

Another ship I recall in my young days was the oil tanker *Georgia*. She had broken in half near Haisbro' Sands. I had been ill in bed with measles or some such illness so was recuperating when Dad came to warn Mother not to worry if she heard the maroons. The fishermen had been watching a vessel off Beeston Hill and thought the lifeboat would have to launch. At my request to go and see what was going on, I was quickly told, 'You can't go down there, you've been ill abed!' So I had to be content to stay indoors and await developments. The fishermen evidently launched to her assistance, but it turned out to be half of a boat, the other half lying on the sandbank off Cromer with the men still on board. The Cromer lifeboat launched and was able to save all of the men. The seepage of oil from the stricken vessel came in on the tide for many weeks, bringing ashore many seabirds covered in thick tar and oil. My friend Margaret and I scoured the beaches for these helpless birds, but it was of no use - our efforts were in vain.

5. Earning a Living

Average family earnings in my youth were about £1 or 30/- old money per week. Boys worked as errand boys in their spare time, delivering goods. Paper boys earned about 5/-. My brother Bob worked for Mr Bertram Watts in the early mornings when he was not at school. He was glad to go caddying on the golf links, as most of his chums did, but I remember him saying how mean some of the golfers were - 'threepenny tippers and tanner tippers'! He managed to put together an old cycle which he had acquired for a few shillings. Mr Prince, the caddy master, was not too well liked by the boys who needed to earn a few pence; he would keep boys waiting about, never to earn a penny all day.

When the Town Council made arrangements for stones to be picked from the beaches and sent away to the potteries by rail, it was looked upon as a possible disaster as the town would lose its defence against the elements on the storm-lashed sea front, but on the other hand it was a great source of revenue and provided work for the many unemployed at that time. In the winter fishermen and others looked on this as a valuable supplement to their income. They did not receive unemployment money. I think it was about 1934-5 when stone-picking first began, and many thousands of tons of stones were removed eventually from the beaches. A special kind of 'blue' flint was required and these were then weighed and sent by rail to Stoke-on-Trent for china.

To see the men, young and old, engaged on this was to be reminded of so many convicts, strung out along the beach, working from the west of the present lifeboat slipway to beyond Beeston Hill. They would be crouched down, backs against the northerly gales, in rain, hail or snow, to earn a mere pittance. Every type of receptacle was used to transport their peds of stones to the weigh-in point near the Grand Hotel. Here a foreman or 'ganger' would sit in a wooden hut and await the workmen and check over their stones. He would have a large weighing machine and each ped of stones was weighed, noted and checked. Unsuitable stones would be discarded as useless. Records were kept and they were paid at the end of the week. They got twopence ha'penny for a ped weighing about six stone. Most of the men averaged about £1 or £1. 5s. - the foreman's wage was £1. 10s.

Carrying the peds of stones up the Marble Arch slope. c. 1931

All sorts of contraptions were made by the men and the boys to convey their stones from where they had picked them to the check point: prams, pushchairs, go-carts, barrows large and small, old bikes transformed with trailers behind. They would come in all sizes and shapes along the promenade, up the Marble Arch slopes to the top. Some enterprising groups would find a way of conveying several peds of stones on trolleys, only to find the weight of the stones too much for the wheels and they would buckle under, often collapsing. Many prams and puschairs didn't make it, leaving utter confusion on the promenade. I well remember old 'Tooffee' Farrow having a large old-fashioned pram which his good lady, Arabella,

...stones and all hurtled skywards.

had bought at a 'jumble' for him. It had huge wheels and a hood in which he had got his load of stones. Negotiating the slope on the West Prom, one of the wheels suddenly careered off and the pram, stones and all, hurtled skywards, 'Tooffee' hanging on for dear life.

Many of my brother's friends were engaged on this work as well as fathers brothers and uncles. A teenager at the time, I would go to one of his chums, Jimmy 'Chibbles' Bishop, who lived in the Avenue with his wife Alison and baby Janet, collect a flask of hot coffee or cocoa with some buns, then to my Aunt Bessie whose husband also needed sustenance. Several flasks of hot drink were installed in Janet's pram and I would push her along the promenade, never knowing in which direction they would be engaged in finding flints. They would then all assemble in a shelter or lee of a breakwater and consume their victuals.

Somewhere around 1936, my father was brought home one day, carried on the arms of some of his fellow workers after he had tried to hobble home. It seems that as he was 'crowding' his barrow round the icy prom, he had slipped and now was in considerable pain. His ankle had immediately swollen up and it was difficult to get his boot off. The doctor was called in and he expressed the opinion that it was badly sprained and gave some advice which Mother followed. Several days later the ankle was giving a great deal of trouble and Dad was in agony and none too happy. Jack 'Tar' Bishop then arrived to look at it and give his opinion. He was the football trainer and often attended to strains etc. His opinion was the same - bad sprain. This went on for about three weeks.

In all this time, Father had been sleeping on the old sofa in the living room, unable to negotiate the stairs to bed. Each day Mother had been using horse oils and linament to massage the swollen limb. In much pain and discomfort Father had protested, but the doctor, calling in fairly often, said that as it was so swollen it would take some time. Several fishermen called in with their usual comments! Busy with helping Mother, I had been spring cleaning the little scullery area one morning and was hanging wallpaper when Dr Beaton arrived. Taking one look at the bad foot he said to Father, 'Let's have a look at your other foot, West, and compare them. This one certainly seems out of shape.' Whereupon Mother got down to remove the sock. 'Oh dear,' she said apologetically, 'I'm afraid this one doesn't look as if it's had a wash lately.' She had been too busy looking after the one foot - the other was forgotten. Wearing a black sock, the foot nearly matched it!

Dr Beaton decided an X-ray at Cromer hospital was necessary and the ambulance arrived to take him there. A message finally came to say he had got to have an operation to reset the broken bones. During the weeks he had lain on the couch, the three broken bones had set. He was a very long while in plaster, his whole leg being encased up to the knee. He must have had at least a year walking about on crutches and managed to wear through two or three metal supports in the base of the plaster.

Father was quite fed up with the inactivity all this while, but Mr Dennis the butcher, who had a shop in Co-op Street, offered to take him with him in his van to market once or twice a week. He thoroughly enjoyed all this and would often bring home a chicken or two, or rabbits and suchlike, for Mother to cook. One day he had been in the same butcher's shop, where the usual customers would collect of an evening, when someone mentioned that the spurs on the cockerel's legs were worth 2/6d each. He came home very hurriedly and told Mother this, saying,

'Mary Ann where did you put those old spurs off the fowls we had?'

'Spurs,' she said, 'whatever do you want them for?'

'They're worth half-a-crown each, so they say in the butcher's.'

'Well I think I put them in the muck-tub (dustbin), they won't be any good now.'

When he finally came back home again, Mother was curious as to the outcome.

'Well,' she said, 'how much did you get?'

'Nothing,' he said, 'that b........lot were pulling my leg!' But he took it all in good part. I don't think it was April Fool's day either.

Later on, when he was fully recovered, he was foreman for the Council at the stone-picking weigh-in and earned 30/- a week.

Whilst boys were caddying or running errands, girls were going into service or to work in the hotels which employed quite a few people. The large hotels of that day, the Grand, the Burlington and Sheringham Hotel, catered for the gentry who were now coming to the coast for holidays, golf and sailing on the Broads. They stayed in the hotels whilst their chauffeurs, nannies and maids stayed in the smaller houses. Many boarding houses were doing very good business, as most families who came would often stay for a month or longer. It was a time for many households to welcome visitors, as it meant a better standard of living. Although lots of cottages were small, they would manage to accommodate two or three guests. At that time they would vacate bedrooms and make space for holiday-makers. It was a time of 'apartments', not the 'bed and breakfast' era which followed. This meant that families would hire a sitting room, one or two bedrooms, whichever was available, use of bathroom and toilet for about £1 or £1 10s. per week. £1 10s. was the usual price paid for a sitting room, same for each bedroom - this would be at the height of the season. For this money, the landlady would do all the cooking required from early morning until late at night. The family would purchase the necessary meat, vegetables and fruit and then specify what meals they would require to be served for breakfast, lunch, afternoon tea and dinner. Some meals would be three or four courses, so she certainly earned the money.

Many families came year after year and we would look upon them almost as friends. On the other hand, you also got the very mean types who would stretch the provisions and expected landladies to work miracles with the tiniest amount of food. My mother, like many others, was glad to let her rooms. As it was a small house, she could only let one bedroom and the sitting room, and to do this was quite a nightmare. All the clothes were removed from the wardrobe in the bedroom, and the cupboards and drawers, and had to be

Ena with her charges, Martin and Annabel Williamson, East Prom. 1927

found a place somewhere else Probably when we were young it might have been less of a problem, but when we were older, it was difficult, to say the least! My sister Ena slept at Grandmother's in Beeston Road, so that made one less, but she was in service by then anyway. Father never felt entirely happy when visitors arrived, although he would show them a very welcome attitude. He preferred his home to be a place where he could do as he liked. We only had one toilet and this presented many problems when Father was in a hurry. Mother would say, 'Willie, you'll have to wait, the visitors are using it.' His reply was usually 'Blast the visitors!' Yet all in all, both my parents made the visitors feel very much at home. Mother was a good cook and could turn her hand to anything. Father often brought home lovely lobsters, crabs and fish and Mother would offer these to any special family that we liked, with no extra charge. Many times have I served afternoon high tea with a dish of lovely red lobsters, just as a special treat.

Early in the year, letters and enquiries would arrive and rooms booked with a deposit of a few shillings. As the dates required were taken a hectic exchange of letters would begin trying to fit in the various families until all the weeks from May to October were filled. We had many who came year after year, and often these families made lasting friendships on the beaches and cliffs of Sheringham so that they would try to plan their next year's holiday and all arrive together. At the same time they booked their tents on the beach adjacent to each other, usually from Jimmy Dumble or Jimmy Scotter. They often preferred the West End beach, just below the Grand Hotel.

We had some very nice people, the Pestalls from Woodford Essex, and then there were the Laskeys from Loughton and Shepherds from Leicester. They nearly always came at the same time for two or three weeks. I always enjoyed this time most of all, for my mother allowed me to wait at table and clear away. She was busy cooking and dishing into tureens and dishes ready for me to take in, so my job was to set the tables with clean starched linen, clean all the silver and fill the cruet. One job not to my liking was to clean all the steel knives on the knife board on which I would sprinkle some brown powder out of a tin.

As we had no bathroom, only the toilet on the small landing, the bedroom contained wash-stand, basins and other toilet accessories, beside the usual bedroom furniture. Therefore, early in the morning, piping hot water had to be carried up in jugs for washing and shaving. We had no way of heating water except by the old kitchen range. In the early days, I remember Mother had to be up to light it to get the water hot and also to cook all the breakfasts. Often Father had to rise early to go off to the crab and lobster grounds, so the visitors were told not to worry if they heard strange noises in the night, it was only the men of the house preparing for departure. Of course, visitors from the towns and cities were delighted to be in a fisherman's home and would ply Father with all sorts of questions. Being the usual laconic type when it came to talking about his work, he was often a bit reluctant to expound on everyday items that he had lived with all his life. So very often Mother would say,

'Willie, you might have told them people a few more things, they're interested you know.'

'Yes, they might be, but I hen't got toime for that.'

Nevertheless, when 'toime' did permit some evenings, they would be regaled with stories about Old Shuck and suchlike.

A heavy breakfast would start the day, then possibly they would collect all the pails, spades, shrimp nets and balls and make for the beach. Usually the lady of the party would get off to the shops early on those glorious summer mornings. The shops would be full of fresh vegetables and fruit. They didn't have far to go to the barbers, butchers, dairies, fried fish shops and bakeries - the aroma of freshly-baked cakes and bread in the early morning was enough to make anyone hungry. Once they had deposited the goods back home and given instructions for the day, off they could go, knowing full well that when they returned a delicious meal would soon be on the table for them to enjoy.

Lunch would be the usual joint of meat with its vegetables, followed by fruit tarts and custard. I would serve the first course and then they would ring a little bell and platters and dishes would be brought out and pudding, creams and plates would be taken in, followed, after another summons on the bell, by a large pot of tea. Often the visitors would keep me chattering and Mother didn't always approve of this. She would kindly say, 'You can't keep in there - I need you to help me'. Another time she would correct me if I didn't say the words that I should have. Such as when visitors said how much they had enjoyed their meal and would I thank Mother, I replied 'Right you are!' This was certainly frowned upon and I was told to say something like 'Thank you very much', or just 'Yes, thank you'.

I don't remember getting a wage at all in those early years, but at the end of the summer, I would go off to Norwich where a new school outfit was bought, new winter coat and shoes and a very smart blazer. This, I supposed, was the accepted procedure. I never questioned it. As I hadn't yet left school, I was quite happy to receive some nice tips now and again when people left, or sometimes a lovely gift. Once Mr and Mrs Pestall and Betty, their daughter, were returning home. Beside the kitchen window was a very nice cycle. It was a second-hand one and had cost £1. When asked if I liked it, I replied 'Oh yes, it's lovely' thinking it had been bought for Betty and they were taking it home on the train. I was overcome with joy when they said it was mine. They had bought it for me! Joy of joys! My own bike! Another year it was a tennis racquet. When they came each year we became great friends and often they would invite me to join them on the beach in their tent which held all the paraphernalia for making afternoon tea. When the visitors booked a tent on the beach, I was delighted as this gave me a bit more time for my own pleasures. All my friends were enjoying the beach and the sea whilst I was having to make sure I was at home for all meals to serve at table. No sooner did a meal end than we were preparing for another - and the stacks of washing up, pans, dishes and glassware! Some visitors preferred to come home for afternoon tea, especially if they were elderly, but all finished the day with an evening meal and we were often washing up at 11 o'clock at night - all for 30/- a week. Just imagine a boiling hot kitchen range on a hot summer's day! Later Mother had a luxury item and installed a gas oven - what bliss!

Of course at the same time, the menfolk had to be fed after their long haul at sea. They would embark after eating bacon and eggs which one could smell cooking in the early hours, to return at dawn to hot rolls, tea and toast. Fortunately we lived very near the Co-op bakery where all the bread, pastries and cakes were cooked for the Co-op Stores opposite. Into those large ovens, fuelled by blazing fires below, went everything, roasts, tarts, and pies brought in by several families. Landladies found this a great boon and one could see them hurrying along in their pinafores or aprons, carrying trays of meat, pies and so on. The only identification was a slip of paper with one's Co-op number on, and this would be tucked into the side of a pastry crust visible to the baker and owner. My mother was grateful for this amenity as she not only cooked all the food for the visitors, but my father and brother liked their prune tarts, meat pies, roasts and especially home-made bread. All this could never have been accommodated in the old range or gas cooker, so I would be sent with various assortments on a tray and then required to collect at about one o'clock. Then one would

hurrying along...
carrying trays of meat
and pies...

watch the bakers fetching out items on their long-handled ladles on to the huge spotless table near by. A search amongst the goodies would begin. Mother's number was 551. If I identified them, alright, but what happened when the scrap of paper had been slightly burnt? This could happen quite easily and then I would try to distinguish Mother's pie-crust - not always so easy amongst all the dishes. When I got back home she would say, 'That's not mine. I never make patterns round the edge like that', or there was the possibility that what you thought was strawberry tart could be beef patty!

One family that came every year, usually for the month of August, was the Reverend Grantham from Leicestershire. He was always pleased when my father could take him off in the boat for mackerel, dabs, plaice or bass and would avail himself of the opportunity to fish from the boat. Dad would rig up the lines and take sufficient bait along. Of course the weather was not always favourable and, being from the cities and towns, they thought they could go to sea each day. This was certainly not wise if the forecasts were bad. Another factor was the tides; if the men had been off with the early tides for crabs and lobsters, they would have a great deal to do when they got ashore and needed some well-earned rest too, but visitors would make the request to get off on a fine afternoon for fishing. On one such occasion my brother, who was quite adamant about not going, finally had to give in and accompany the party. Now this Reverend was inclined to be mean and would take home all the fish he caught for my mother to cook, some no bigger than the palm of one's hand. They were often so small she would say it was like cooking butterflies, and to say the least she got a bit fed up. She would much rather be off there at sea fishing herself if ever the opportunity occurred, and she would hope to be included in any party that would be 'railing' and 'kipping'. ('Railing' refers to fishing with hand lines held over the stern or sides of the boat whilst the engine is running fairly fast through the water; 'kipping' is the reverse, as the fishing party remains almost stationary over a 'bass' hole or a productive spot.) This day she had her fishing gear ready in record time; it didn't take her long to don her fawn Burberry mackintosh and a beret she kept especially for the occasion.

After they had been at sea a couple of hours, the fishing was slow and Bob, who had been at sea in the early hours, thought they should be heading for home. But the Reverend was still casting his line, so, with a quick flick of his wrist, Bob suddenly tossed the rest of the bait overboard, Mother just seeing him out of the corner of her eye. Father, maybe also aware of the episode, made the remark that they ought to be heading for home. Reverend Grantham looked up, most surprised, still ready to prolong his fishing trip. He glanced around, looking towards Bob who, still holding the bait board, said, 'Well we're out of bait, so we'll het to go home'.

Another time when the family called the Pestalls were with us once again, they too thought they would like to go fishing, and when asked had they been fishing before, 'Oh yes', they said, 'we've been off in ships many times, but not exactly fishing'!

'This isn't the same as the large boats, you know,' said Dad, 'these small boats do plenty of rolling about out there, especially when we find a spot to fish over. You might not feel too good then,' he informed them.

. Anyway it was decided they were going to try it Mrs Pestall turned to me and rather nervously asked if I was going. 'I'll be alright if you go' she said. When we set out, the sea was beautifully calm, the tide on the ebb, just leaving the stones - we knew it was going to be a lovely afternoon. In the boat was Father, Bob, Mother, Mr and Mrs Pestall and myself. We all had our lines which Bob and Father were busily were busily baiting up, ready to steer for a 'bass' hole, or well-known spot where the boat would 'swilk' backwards and forwards, engines stopped and swinging with the tide. The hot sun poured down on our heads. With the added smell of the petrol fumes plus the bait, it wasn't long before Mrs P., looking pale, turned to me and whispered, 'May, are you alright?' evidently hoping I wasn't. My first thought was 'Oh dear, what's Dad going to say now? I was thoroughly enjoying the afternoon; we had hardly started to fish and now it looked as if it was to be curtailed, so my reply was 'Yes', still hoping. Another half hour passed by and we were now abreast of Beeston Hill, the tide almost at low water. All around were large seaweed-covered rocks, ugly and sharp, becoming more evident and exposed as the tide receded. These lay between us and the shore; we could see and hear families playing there on the beach and they seemed a long way from us. As I looked at Mrs P. she was certainly much greener, and turning to me said she wasn't feeling too good. Could we be put ashore? Rather hesitantly I murmured a few words to Dad, having visions of his anger. How was he going to manoevre the boat amongst all those rocks without running a hole in her? Rather than let poor Mrs P. take all the blame, I thought I had better go with her. Bob and Dad then got the oars and, standing up carefully, pushed the boat through the water. We gradually got near the largest rocks and, hoisting up our dresses, we clambered over the side into very deep water. Somehow we managed to get up on to the rocks and the beach, Mrs Pestall's colour returning almost immediately. The annoying thing was that I had never felt seasick and out there on the calm sea bobbed our fishing party, thoroughly enjoying themselves.

6. An Escapade

As the summer ended and autumn approached, with dark winter evenings ahead, my brother and his fishermen chums would collect together in Mother's warm living room where there was a large kitchen table, suitable for playing cards or dominoes. My Mother was always happy to have them there and often we participated in games of Newmarket, a firm favourite, Housie Housie or Rummy; another one I vaguely remember was called Squiggles. Although the house was small, there would generally be eleven or twelve around the table, and sometimes as many as eighteen or nineteen. How we all managed to get around the table I don't know; chairs would be brought out from the front room and the old settee would seat four or five. There was little money for outside activities, even if these were available, and one couldn't go to the cinema every night of the week, so, with a blazing fire in the hearth, it was all good fun.

On one such night as this, I recall my brother and his chums, myself included as the only girl among several young men, playing a prank that could have had serious consequences. As it was, it all turned out well and remains with me as a memory of happy days.

It was a dark, foggy, November night with a sea mist floating in from the sea; ships were often aground on such a night and it was usual for most of the lads present to go off in the lifeboat. Lots more ships came ashore in those days, quite a regular occurrence. Now one of the lads, Kitchener Pegg, was a strict salvationist and of course would never have played any card games as the others did, but whenever he was off to band practice at the Army, he would find time to come in and have a chat; he was a very clever fellow and could use any musical instrument to the best advantage, belonging to an old Sheringham family, the Peggs, who were always in the forefront when it came to music and singing. This night he called in on us on his way to the barracks a few doors away.

The evening wore on and everyone was thoroughly enjoying the games. About an hour later, we suddenly heard quite clearly the unmistakable sound of a ship's foghorn. Everyone scrambled to their feet, overturning the chairs in the rush for the door; caps and hats, which had previously been tossed on to a picture or hook, were reached for in their haste to be first to get a 'jacket' at lifeboat house if she was needed. The foghorn had sounded so loud that we could, in our imagination, have sworn she was nearly ashore! The table nearly overturned, with cards disbanded in the scramble for hats and coats, pictures hanging askew, as everyone tried to get out of  the back door in a bunch in the mad rush to see who would get to the sea front first.

Pandemonium had reigned for a few minutes as we adjusted our eyes to the murky darkness outside. Suddenly a figure appeared coming up the yard out of the mist, a grin all over his face. He was carrying something in his hand, one of the instruments he had evidently been playing - a clarinet! Of course, to our amazement it was our friend Kitchener who had hidden in Father's shed and had played a very good prank on us by blowing this so realistically, getting us all to leave our sport in the belief that it was a ship's siren. Needless to say, the lads were slightly disappointed. Well the laugh was on us; now he would have a yarn to tell. Finally we realised it was a joke and went indoors. Then someone, I don't remember who it was, suddenly had the bright idea of trying the trick on someone else. Across the road from us lived old Mr Middleton, a fisherman whose nickname was 'Will Eye'. The boys huddled in the alley way beside the cottage where we lived and once more 'Kitch' gave a blow. Again it was so realistic one could almost hear the boat - the yellow fog which hung like a blanket added to the atmosphere. After a few moments we suddenly saw 'Will Eye' appear, pulling on his jacket, as he hurried down the road. This caused us quite some amusement, and all agreed it would be a good idea to see if we could get one of our uncles out and some fishermen who lived almost side by side in Beeston Road. This was Teddy 'Fiddy' West, signalman in the lifeboat, and not many doors away was 'Rally' West. Of course I had to go along to see the fun - a girl with eight or nine boys - none of us realising what it could lead to.

Opposite these cottages in Beeston Road was a small opening which led to other cottages; we stood in here away from the road and 'Kitch' did his party trick. Inside the cottage we could hear my young cousin Joyce shouting for her Dad. 'Dad!' she called from upstairs, 'I think there's a boat close in'. Next thing was Teddy emerging and struggling into his jacket, at the same time shouting for 'Rally'. 'Come on Bob, she sound really close!' The pair then went hurrying towards the sea front, disappearing into the fog.

Another few yards along the same street, and a little way into the alley way known as 'Back Loke', lived, in a tiny cottage, a real Sheringham character, 'Tooshy' Brown, his wife Evelyn, and two very young boys, David and Gordon. 'Tooshy' was a youngish man and a lifeboat man, ever ready to take part in anything to do with the sea; he would be only too eager to get to the cliff to see what was going on. I knew that if he heard this he would go rushing off to find out, so was very determined to try to stop him. But suddenly the cottage door opened and the light shone out; in the beam from the cottage I could see 'Tooshy'. I went forward and clutched him by the arm and said, 'Walter, don't go - it's all a false alarm. It's only your chums playing a trick.' But I could see it was quite hopeless; he brushed me on one side and said, 'Evelyn has gone to the pictures, I'll het to take the boys to Mrs C. - she'll look after them'. No amount of talking could change him, he was too eager to go. I can see him now. He had evidently been braiding a crab pot, his two little boys abed, but scooping up both little boys, one under each arm, he raced off to his old standby in Priory Road.

After this the crowd of us decided to see if we could hoax a few more of our relations and friends. Calling outside a few of the fishermen's houses, we were a little surprised when it didn't get the response we expected. I remember seeing the shadow on the blind at Jimmy 'Paris' West's house; it was the same with John Cooper. We had now reached Beach Road and someone suggested going along the prom as it would be even more realistic, especially if the 'foghorn' was blown near the Tank shelter. The sea I remember was lapping quite calmly on the stones, yellowy grey in the dim light that was thrown by the very few gas lamps. At least it was a calm night and fog thick and heavy on the water - just the kind of night that might see a ship looming off the shore. Enthusiasm now gripped us all as we heard young 'Kitch' do another of his imitations.

The nearest pub was the Crown Inn; this was the usual rendezvous for the coxswain and his mates for their customary pint. Little did we realise that some of the crew might be inside. This was about 1932 and the *J.C.Madge* was housed in her shed about three quarters of a mile across the golf links, difficult to negotiate in daylight, but far worse in the dark, with no lights to guide them. As the last sound of the 'foghorn' drifted away, the doors of the Crown opened and in the beams of light we saw John 'Sparrow' Hardingham, second coxswain, emerging, followed by Bennet Middleton and Jimmy Scotter. The whole thing now took on a serious aspect as we saw them speed away into the gloom. We decided we had better be safe than sorry; all of us were getting a trifle concerned, but no one was going to make the decision to disband and I followed in the wake of the rest. We walked towards the Windham Arms, probably on our way home. Some fishermen came out, my father amongst them, and although he had known about it all along, he was now being taken over by others' enthusiasm as they were all remarking on how close in 'she' was and how they could hear 'her' engines! Imagination was running riot by now and all were for going home to get their boots. In particular two brothers who lived in Whitehall Yard, Stanley Little (Stilly) and Dick, both on their way to the old Hythe, were seen running up Wyndham Street with their heavy boots under their arms, heading for the links and the lifeboat shed.

In Gun Street my grandparents owned a small crab shop. An uncle who was with us had the key of this and thought it would be a good idea if we all got inside to see what was happening across at the Lobster. This was another public house much used by the fishermen. At that moment a large group of fishermen came out of the main door, amongst them were Jimmy Dumble, the coxswain, also 'Corporal' Grice, 'Demon' Cooper and 'Lobster' Farrow, heading for the west gangway. Everybody was now quite sure there was probably going to be trouble and we had better make our way homewards. We knew that there was every chance that a boat might get launched off the beach. My brother was very anxious and said, 'You had better go home, there's going to be trouble if we get found out.' He was concerned that we should all go home and not say a word to anyone about it. Kitchener was still wondering what the outcome would be and said, 'Let's go around by the sea wall, pretend we're courting, then we'll know what's going to happen.' As we went towards the promenade we met my father who very sternly said, 'It's time you went home. I think they're going to launch one of the boats off the gangway and I shall have to go in it.'

When we got to the promenade several of them had congregated under the lamp at the corner; within the light thrown from this lamp were about forty men. It was absolutely fantastic to hear the remarks they were making; they were most excited and some were laying their ears against the sea wall, perfectly sure they could hear 'her' engines. We asked what all the fuss was about. 'She's suffin close in,' said Jimmy Mace Johnson who knew everything, 'just you listen to har, I kin hear har injuns, I think we'd betta lornch.' Just at that crucial moment, along came fisherman Middleton, the first one to be hoaxed, and as he had seen us a couple of hours earlier, we felt sure he would give us away; we awaited his words with apprehension, but he seemed as taken in as all the others and he was just as eager to launch the hoveller off the gangway. By this time they were gradually going down the gangway, my father amongst them. No doubt he thought he had better look willing, or he might have really convinced himself there really was a ship ashore!

We then headed for home after watching the men rowing away into the fog. How far they rowed I never did find out, but I think it was as far as Beeston Hill. The following day my father took me on one side and said, 'You know that was a serious thing you did, all of you, last night. If anyone get to hear about it ther'll be a load of trouble. Don't ever say a word about this or you'll get us all into a scrape with the authorities.' So, for many years, nothing more was said. Then one day Mr 'Paris' West was next to me in the fish shop queue and he quietly said, 'That was a rummun when you nearly launched the lifeboat,' so I knew a few had been talking. We never attempted anything like that again!

The crew of the R.N.L.I. boat the J.C.Madge which served the town between 1904 and 1936. The lady in the centre knitted bright red woollen scarves for all the crew. There was much amusement when the younger ones paraded in Mother's kitchen to try them on. L. to R. back row: Jimmy Dumble (coxswain), Harry 'Munchy' Middleton, James 'Slily' Hannah, 'Old Bennet' Middleton, Charlie 'Chicken' Grice, John 'Sparrow' Hardingham (second cox), H. Cooper, John 'Teapot' West, Henry 'Downtide' West, Stanley 'Stilly' Little, Billy 'Cutty' Craske. In the far background are 'Young Chicken' and Eric Wink. Seated in front are Henry 'Pinny' Little, Bob 'Kiff' Pegg, Bob 'Nesta' West, Walter 'Tooshy' Brown, Jimmy 'Chibbles' Bishop, Alfie 'Seatoad' Cooper. Teddy 'Lux' Craske and 'Reddy' Winn-Middleton. Teddy Craske. on the right of the picture, is the only one alive, now 90 years old.

7. A Close-knit Community

My parents, Henry Willie West and Mary Ann, were both born in Sheringham just as their parents were, and both descended from fisher folk. Like many who were born in the village of those days, they would often tell me about Sheringham and how it was, its characters, its way of life. A close-knit community in which most families were related to one another- they didn't marry 'foreigners', as they were often referred to, and looked upon any stranger that walked into the village as a 'foreigner'. That unfortunate intruder was often stoned and jeered at.

How long the nickname of 'Shannocks' has applied to local-born people is hard to say, and the origin is obscure. They were well known all along the coast as the 'Mad Shannocks' as their reputation for being wild and reckless grew. They would fight at the drop of a hat, and sometimes were avoided. To 'shanny' means to be wild, run about recklessly, and in all probability this is how the word derived. They took great risks, especially when they went to sea. They sailed far from these shores in search of cod, ling, and skate, and also went whaling off the coasts of Iceland. Proud, independent, of a superstitious nature, determined and hardworking, strictly religious, rugged and colourful characters, whose pride was in their boats and homes. My parents always regarded a true Shannock as one born in the town, of Sheringham-born parents. The days I am speaking of were before the First World War. After that, with the influx of folks during that time, a true Shannock became rarer.

Whenever I had the time to spare, it was enlightening to listen to them both tell tales and yarns of their youth and describe quite vividly what the little village was like when they were young and its old characters and traditions. How I wish now that I had had the use of a tape recorder, for Father could tell a tale with no gross exaggeration, but with a reality and vividness so that one could visualise the scene. Mother, not to be outdone, would chime in every so often with contradictory statements of dates and places, just to put the matter straight! But she had tales to tell too, mostly of the land and how she helped the various men-folk who worked for her father on the fields he rented from the Upcher family.

Many yards abounded in the village of 1890; most were called after the families who lived in them, or who had built the cobbled stone cottages. Most of these yards have long since disappeared into modern development, but some were still there in my youth. A few remain, such as Angel Yard, Whitehall Yard, Barcham's Yard and Chapman's Yard, but Cox's Yard, where Mother was born, has long gone. This was situated behind West's fish shop and the Music shop. There were three or four dwellings here and quite a few of the Cox family lived in them at one time. Just further down the High Street was Upcher's Yard; one went through an archway into it and the arch is still there, but the three little cottages have gone. Here had lived a few of the old ones, some I clearly remember, Old Joe 'Bottle' Farrow and Mary 'Tearny' Pegg. In one was my father's Aunt Mary (Kerrison) and I would call to see her when a child. She always cooked lovely gingerbread and we children would sit and listen to her tales. Her little home was spotlessly clean. Here too had lived my great grandfather, Robert 'Philloo' Cooper, in the latter part of his life, but of course he died before I was born.

My father was born at Welcome Cottage, No. 4, Gun Street, in 1885. This was a row of cottages so close one could touch each side quite easily, which ended with a yard called

Tantivy. This was known as Tantivy Loke. All of these little dwellings had an outside toilet opposite them. Gun Street was a private road at one time, owned by the Cox family who lived at the little shop on Lifeboat Plain and also in one of the cottages. A chain was put across the lane once a year on Boxing Day. Gun Street was not so much a street, really as a yard, and washing was strung across it from cottage to toilets. Earlier it had been called Lobster Lane and led down to the Gun Plain, but I have heard that it was called Pocket Handkerchief Square after the pocket handkerchieves worn on the heads of some of the old women who sat in their kitchen doorways.

Dad and Mum would describe the little cobblestone cottages which lined each side of the High Street, with their white painted railings and little gardens full of flowers. There were only a few streets when they were young. My mother would describe the haystacks, fields and hedges on the corner of what is now Augusta Street. She was once stoned at this corner by some boys who were hiding in the 'deek' as she called it. They broke her nose and she always had a scar there to remind her as the doctor had had to put stitches in. There were fields to the westwards of the main street. A farm yard owned by Mr Upcher ran through to a farm gate situated near the present Woolworth's store. Cattle would be brought across to the town's reservoir or driven home to the village at Upper Town by his team man. Of course the Town Clock, built in 1862, was one of the meeting places for the folks to collect their water in pails or sometimes carrying yolks on their shoulders. It was the obvious place to chat and exchange news. Horses would be brought here to be watered. This being the main water supply for the town, it was the centre point of the village and was still used for horses even in my youth and beyond. Many years later it was modernised as we see it today. I have heard Father say it was the site of the village stocks although there were others, one near the Dunstable Arms pub and another at the crossroads leading out of Sheringham near the Holway Road.

There was another site for getting water adjacent to Lusher's Bakery. This was known as the Polk and a couple of steps led down to it; Pump Yard was near by. Most of the cottagers in this area would use this fresh water supply - they had no other means of getting water for general use.

Upper Sheringham, or Upper Town as most locals know it, was the main village and most folks of Lower Town were baptised and married there. When it came to being buried in the grave yard, they were carried on the shoulders of the fishermen to their final resting place, with all the family mourners walking from one village to the other. This was before the coming of the railway and Mother would say how lonely it was as the last houses in Lower Town were near Water Bank Road, and after that just a lane or cart-track to Upper Town with fields and hedges on all sides.

The boundary of Beeston Regis and Sheringham was provided by the beck which flowed freely from the Spring Woods, over the Common and down Back Loke as it made its way to the sea. At one time, in my parents' day, it flowed all the way above ground, down Beeston Road to the culvert on the beach. Later, of course, this was covered over and diverted through several gardens. Folks who lived east of this beck attended the church over Beeston Hill and were mostly married and buried there. Beeston Road was first called Paper Mill Road or Lane. Here had stood a tiny watermill, probably ancient and still in existence in 1850.

The Beeston Infants' School was built in 1875 at the lower end of this road which was known as Old School Corner; here the children of the main village and Beeston attended.

They began at a very early age, some at two and a half, others at three. The beck flowed close by and the children of this tiny school would often find this more compelling than the lessons. There was one headmistress and an occasional pupil teacher who would devote themselves to the welfare of the children. At the age of eight they progressed to the school at Upper Sheringham, a walk of a mile and a quarter.

A lane leading from Bridge Street and Paper Mill Lane led all the way to Beeston church and this was called Woodhouses Lane. Mill Lane, now Beeston Road, got its name from the paper mill which stood on the corner of the Avenue. How long the mill has been in existence is hard to say, but there is mention of a water mill in Sheringham being owned by an Adam Brown in 1390 - presumably this is the same one. It was in use, employing two men, in 1788 and was quite a productive mill. It had several owners through the years: Mr Bond 1792, Mr Valentine Blyth between 1797 and 1803, Mr Critoph and his widow 1808, Mr Burrell in 1810 and Mr Clark in 1861 employing two men. The last one we are able to ascertain was old John Warbey in 1896. Later this became two cottages, one named Mill Cottage, but sadly it is not so named today.

Today we see Co-operative Street as a quiet thoroughfare, but in my youth it was one of the main shopping streets. My parents said it was earlier called The Piggery owing to its being a lane that led between pigstyes and old sheds on its way to Farmer Olley's barn at its lower end. There was a pond, with chickens and ducks, and the stream fed this on its way to the sea, the beck here being quite dangerous especially at night with no street lamps. There was a tall bank on each side of the beck and a bridge to cross it at the junction of Wyndham Street and Woodhouses Lane. Another bridge was further down Beach Road, the only means of access from the little cottages here across to Lifeboat Plain. The first shop in Lower Sheringham was on Lifeboat Plain and belonged to the Cox family. My mother was one of this family and she used to say that her grandparents, Robert and Ann Cox, had it. Certainly it was run by members of that family and changed hands a few times. Mother would say that all manner of things could be purchased here, from delicate china and glass to lamp oil, tallow candles and general stores.

Near by in Beach Road was a whelk copper and storehouse owned by the Teddy 'Fiddy' West family. Here the fishermen and wives would gather to mend the nets. Young children were employed to do this and also in rope-making. The fish, as it was landed and brought up the beach, was auctioned here and bought by various fish merchants of the day. When bidding started, all very informally, the deal was often clinched by the striking of two stones together and the transaction was completed. It was exactly the same procedure when fish was auctioned on the West End gangway.

A large carpenter's shed owned by 'Money Ben' Johnson stood in Beach Road. Mostly fishermen lived in the tiny cottages on the east side which led up to the cliff edge, and here the nets were stretched out to dry and be mended. In one of the cottages, which were only two-up and two-down, lived Richard Cox and his wife Mary. This was my great-great-grandfather and he had seven sons and two daughters. All of these sons became fishermen and lifeboatmen. Richard was one of the few men who could read and write and had been born in Lower Sheringham in 1803. He was paid 4/- per week to read the Bible to people in their cottages. Although a fisherman, he would journey about the country with his son David, preaching and singing. One of his sons, John my great-grandfather, married Elizabeth Cooper and they lived in Gun Street. He had three sons and three daughters, his sons all going to sea for a living. But he had to bear the sad loss of two of these sons: one,

Richard Cox (in the top hat), born 1803, with his seven sons in 1878.
All became fishermen. Some went to Whitstable, some to Wells.

Robert Henry, off Bacton in 1909, and his other son John, aged 18, whom he found early one morning washed ashore after his boat had overturned in a sudden squall. He was buried in Upper Sheringham.

Also living at the 'Mo' in Beach Road was a Mr Digby-Piggott. He was always coming out of his house complaining of the dirty water and rubbish accumulating in the beck which passed his house. It didn't take the locals long to find him a nickname ,'Old Dirty Waters'. He was never known by anything else after that!

The small alleyway which led from the High Street to the Westcliffe area was called by some folks Slipper's Loke. Others knew it as Fanny's Corner. On the right hand side was the chapel of ease provided by the Reverend Upcher and used by the local fishermen - a chapel much used after wrecks at sea, where the survivors of a storm would offer up their thanks to almighty God for deliverance and a safe return to their loved ones. It was here that the crew of the *Ispolen,* wrecked in 1897, met to offer up their prayers in a service conducted by the Reverend Upcher. The chapel was often used later as a church hall for lifeboat dinners, Oddfellows meetings and later as an auction hall. Many festive occasions to mark an event or an anniversary were held here. Later on this was pulled down to make way for a block of flats.

On the same side of the road, further along, were some small cottages, one of which was used as a dame school for gentlefolk run by Mr Robert Pigott Long and his wife, Martha. The charge was 6d per week. His nickname was 'Old Pa Wagg' Long. He was a devout

Robert Henry Cox, son of John Cox, drowned, July 1909. (Note the gansey)

methodist and church-goer. Like most folks they had little education, but were remarkable in the manner of improving their reading and writing. His father, also Robert Long became coxswain of the *Augusta* lifeboat and corresponded with the Honourable Mrs Upcher at the Hall, writing superb letters and a carefully written account of the service of the boat he was so proud to be in charge of. He was held in high esteem by the Hon. Mrs Charlotte Upcher and all her family and made regular visits to the Hall. Nevertheless he never forgot his position in their service.

On West Cliff itself were many sheds and a collection of small cottages occupied by fishermans' families. In those early days most of the village was involved with fishing and over a hundred boats would leave these shores. Girls and boys were employed on the ropegrounds from an early age to mend nets and braid. Boys began a very early life at sea, some from the age of twelve, it being a tradition to follow their fathers to sea. And it was here, on the cliff edge, that the second private lifeboat, *Henry Ramey* was built. Just a little to westward were the old whelk coppers. All catches of whelks were brought here by the whelk boats which landed their supply at the bottom of Admiralty slipway. Nets of these boats were washed and boiled in the coppers by the Grice brothers. 'Old Man' Grice and his sons would be in charge. Later on I remember Ernie Grimes. As children we would gather there as the hot whelks were winched up out of their coppers. That was the time to eat a few if one was lucky, straight from the coppers, freshly cooked and never tough. Then they were transported by donkey and cart to the railways and all parts.

Going back to my parents' description of the High Street in those days, they would say that a Mr Nightingale started the first bank and lent money; this was in a small house, (now the premises of the present Barclay's Bank) under the management of Mr Fitch. There were some larger houses near the present bank, most of which were owned by Mr Ben Johnson. He was known as 'Money Ben' and would also lend money, often being involved with various beneficial projects. At the rear of this building was another yard called 'Money Ben's Yard'. The Johnson family were a relatively old family, some connected with the sea, but mostly with business projects. Nearly all the cottages on each side of the road had small walls or garden fences. There was no lighting at all anywhere and everywhere would be quite dark. The streets were not made up and one could only find the way by the light shed by the oil lamps within the cottage windows when the occupants were still about their business. 'Such and such a person haven't gone to bed yet!' they would remark. Or prayer meetings would be going on in the little houses and chapels - they would be praying and singing quite loudly.

Further down High Street on the left, was a General Store and Post Office, the first in Sheringham run by a Mr Barcham and his daughter Maria. The rear of these premises became Barcham's yard. My father would relate the story of a serious fire which occurred on these premises one night. This was before he was married and courting Mother, somewhere about 1905 or 6. People ran out of the cottages to find the houses in that area ablaze and the horse-drawn fire engine with its crew dashing on to the scene. They then tried to obtain water from the Polk to put out the fire, rescuing the daughter and her father. Old Mr Barcham acquired the nickname 'Tin Britches'! Another person had a peculiar nickname; he lived a few doors away and was known as 'Smooth Eye'. His real name was Smith and he owned a small sweet shop, just further along towards the sea. The boys would be forever climbing up the little iron railings to peer in at his sweets in the window. He had a great array of goodies which they couldn't afford, but they would gaze in at them with wonder. He would come out and chase them away and if he could get hold of any of them they would feel the back of his hand.

Opposite this was a very pretty little cottage which faced the sea. It had railings all round it, with a flower garden and a green painted porch over the door. Here lived old Tom Cooper and his wife. Nowadays this is the Matella Craft shop, but once it was the Post Office Telephone exchange.

As far as the cliffs, on both sides, were similar types of cottages. Very few are left today, but the present Two Lifeboats pub is very much the same as it was then. It was called the Temperance Hotel when it was run by old Jumbo Gray and was known as the 'Coffee House'. The fishermen met here on a Saturday night to reckon up their week or month's takings. They would work out the shares for crew and boat and another share of the takings as 'Christ's Dole'. It was a regular meeting place. Next door to this was the Mission Room, a wooden building at the north side of the Two Lifeboats, run very efficiently and organised by the Misses Blanche and Emily Pigott of the Upcher family. They took a great deal of interest in the poor and fishing families of the parish, so they organised prayer meetings for the young men. The Mission Room served a very useful purpose, for whenever ships came ashore in those early days, or were wrecked off the coast, this was the haven to which survivors would be brought and given warm clothing and shelter. There would be a blazing fire, warmth and hospitality for any stranded seamen until they could be returned to their homes.

It was here that the crew of the *Ispolen* were taken in 1897 after their brig capsized directly off the town. My father could recall this - he was then twelve years old - seeing her sail in to the shore and the crew being rescued by the lifeboat. He afterwards climbed up to the railings of the Mission and peered into the windows. The men were all seated around a roaring fire, wrapped in blankets, whilst outside the storm and gale were breaking the Norwegian brig to pieces. Mother could recall this event too, quite vividly. As she was crossing the area near the Lobster Inn, struggling against the blizzard which was raging towards the cliff edge with many others, the brig was being blown on shore. Suddenly the masts and rigging collapsed and the vessel, only a few yards from the shore was overwhelmed in the surf. The day before this disaster, the slipway of the lifeboat house on Lifeboat Plain had been washed away, with the cliffs and part of the Crown Inn damaged. So it seemed impossible to launch the *William Bennett* but the R.N.L.I. men decided they were definitely going to get the *William Bennett* into the water somehow. The *Henry Ramey Upcher* boat was hurriedly launched from the West End gangway by the many fishermen there. Heavy snow was on the ground and the roads were like ice, but the R.N.L.I. men were determined and the boat was manhandled from her house on Lifeboat Plain, up Gun Street and into Wyndham Street. These streets were very narrow and on her way, said Mother, she ran into 'Old Smooth Eye's window causing a lot of damage also to the corner of one of the cottages near Beach Road. Unfortunately she wasn't able to rescue the crew of the brig, but her eight men were safely landed by the private lifeboat. Some of the wreckage from the brig was auctioned on the beach a week later, but half her remains can be seen today, on the west side of the Upcher's Groyne, when there has occurred an easterly scour by the tide, shifting the sand which covers her and revealing her remains.

The Norwegian brig Ispolen, built at St Magnus, Bremerhaven, Germany in 1865 and then called the Falk, re-named Ispolen in 1890, material wood, size 240 Brt. According to Lloyd's List she came ashore at Lower Sheringham on January 23rd, 1897 at 3.30p.m. By the following day she had gone to pieces, her 'cargo of ice scattered along the coast'. The crew were saved. Two houses built in Holway Road, Sheringham, shortly after this were named Ispolen and Commodore, their names being painted in glass panels over the doors. The houses still stand, but the glass panels have been removed in later years.

8. Father's Story

My father, Henry William West, was born at No. 4 Gun Street, Sheringham, the home of his grandparents, on November 22nd 1885. He lived here until he was five years old when his parents had a fairly large house built in Beeston Road. It had five bedrooms , a large front room, another large dining room, kitchen, good-sized larder and scullery with a spacious hall and two stair-cases, a far cry from the cottage of two up and two down! The young family moved here in the 1890s, but we must let him tell his tale...

I think I had better start at the beginning with my early days in the little cottage in Gun Street. My parents, Joshua Henry West and his wife Sarah, lived here after their marriage when my grandparents moved to a cottage in Station Road. The first years of my life were spent in this little house, but as it was very close to the main street I was always getting out, and various folks were forever bringing me back again, so my mother thought the safest place for me was the little school in Beeston Road. So she approached the mistress who agreed to take me. I was just three years old when I started. I remember the first thing they gave me to do was knitting - I soon learnt that, but plain knitting was all I did for the first year or so.

All the children of the village and of Beeston went to this little school; the beck flowed close by and we could sail our bits of wood and paper boats here, often getting our feet wet. When I was there a Miss Alice Parnell was the governess and we had some pupil teachers (one was a Miss Skipper) - they were often from the local families and worked hard. When we reached seven or eight years old we had to go to Upper Town school, quite a distance to walk, about one mile and a half daily. This wasn't so bad in the fine weather, but when conditions were bad it wasn't much fun. We would have to get there when snow was deep on the ground, even in blizzards, gales of wind and driving rain, but our fathers would sometimes take us on their backs if the weather kept them from sea. But mostly we got there somehow, carrying our food in bags or baskets. We had to eat this in the playground, not an ideal place when one's dinner was wet. Often we were wet through when we got there. In the dark winter days we left school early to get home before dark. There was no housing at all along the lane that led from Lower Town to Upper Town, just hedges and trees which met overhead. Before the railway was built the last houses in our village were near Waterbank Road. I well remember a trick I once played on the master. My mother always packed my dinner in a red spotted handkerchief to carry to school. One day I dipped my dinner in the village reservoir near the church gates, telling the headmaster that it had got wet in the rain. When he heard this he promptly sent me home. But I tried this trick once too often, for one day after dipping my food in the water at the reservoir and telling the same story, Mr Savage said 'Well West, you can eat your dinner, whether it is wet or not, 'cause I see you today dipping your dinner and you're not getting away with it this time!'.

Our day would begin at eight o'clock and end at four. There were seven standards in all and when you reached the seventh you left. One of my friends was Graham Savage, the son of the headmaster, and almost the same age as myself. We got along very well together and were good friends. He passed several scholarships, one to Cambridge University where he gained first class honours. After serving as an officer in the First World War, he returned to education and became an inspector of schools, finally becoming chief inspector of schools for all England. He brought great honour to the little school we went to; I think he was knighted by the Queen for his long service to education.

I left school when I reached the last class and could not get any higher. I think I was about twelve or thirteen years old. Most of the boys went to sea for a living as I was about to do, but first of all I went caddying on the golf links which had been recently opened. It wasn't the grand place it is today. When it was first laid out it only had nine holes and we had to go round the course twice. There was no caddy master and we had to take whatever money was offered to us. If we were lucky enough to go round the links twice, we got eightpence, that was old money, or a sixpenny tip. Sometimes we got a tuppenny tip.

Another job I did was to clean the boots and shoes of the gentlemen who stayed at the hotels and carry their golf clubs. Some very well-known gentlemen of those days who came to live at Sheringham were the Right Honourable Augustine Birrell, Member of Parliament and Chief Secretary for Ireland, and Ben Davis, the Welsh tenor.

I well remember a Mr James Braid and a Mr Taylor playing at Sheringham and I was lucky enough to caddy for Mr Braid, but he was beaten 5 and 4 to play; the day before at Cromer links it was the reverse. I was very fond of golf and later became a member of the club, so you see I enjoyed my caddying days although we didn't earn much.

Then my days at sea started. I was fifteen when my father started to takle me to sea and this was the usual custom. Most of the families followed in the footsteps of the previous generations. Practically every household had someone who went to sea; three parts of the population of the village were fishing families and naturally sons were expected to follow suit - there was little else to do. My father was a very strong man and expected me to have the experience he had and to be able to work as he did. Many times when I got home I would cry and tell my mother, but it did little good. She knew that I had to learn it the hard way and she couldn't afford to be otherwise. I loved the sea, but found it hard to keep up to him; each day I learnt a bit more, and gradually gained his approval. The sea can be a cruel task master, but demands our respect.

But before I tell of my days at sea, I would like to tell you of the first day when I went caddying with my cousin, John Long. He was a bit older than me and quite used to the work, so he thought he would show me the ropes as it was all strange to me. When we got to the links he quickly told me to carry the other lady's clubs. He was caddying for General Davidson's sister and my lady was Mrs Stopford, wife of Colonel Stopford. (Later he was killed in the Boer War crossing the Modder River.) This particular day Mrs Stopford said, after she had played eighteen holes, she was not going round any more, but would pay me my dues if I would run with a letter to the Hall at Upper Sheringham for the Upcher family. I was of course very happy to do this as it meant I would earn one whole shilling and fourpence, the first money I ever earned and was able to take home to my mother. Cousin John was a little put out.

Now I will continue of my early days at sea. Those days were very hard at first, but gradually I became stronger and I thank God that before long I was able to beat my father at hauling the crab and lobster pots. In the winter months we went longer to sea for whelks, then it would be laying lines for cod, and off many hours for herring. Each had its season though sometimes there would be little to earn. Of course it was rowing and sailing in those early days; hauling the boats up and down the beaches, men would handle the boats by slipping their arms into the rowlock and lifting the boats over the sands. There were no mechanical aids; later on hand winches and later still electrical winches were installed.

Young visitors put their questions to Grandfather 'Joyful' (in the boat) and Tom 'Gayton' Cooper. East Beach.

About this time a few large boats got fitted out with engines and I decided to join some younger men, so it meant leaving my father. We had a big new boat built. This boat had an engine installed and it was wonderful to be able to get out to the pots or lines. It seemed like another world after all the hard labour that rowing entailed, sailing against the wind and tide; these engines made our work so much lighter, although we still had to haul our boats up the beaches and carry our gear and nets. When we went off for whelks we would be gone all day because the whelk grounds were a long way off, a nasty situation if the weather worsened as it could so easily on this coast. Then we would have to leave our gear quickly. Most of the boats had their engines installed by a local business man as many of us had not got the money to supply our own. Although the boats got the benefit of the engine installed, those boats that had agreed to this were then tied boats, having to supply their catches at reduced prices to him. There being little alternative, more and more boats resorted to this as time went on. Well anyway I was quite happy with my two partners and we never had any quarrels. Around this time, 1909, my father had a boat built called *Premier*. I thought this was in honour of Loyd George, but find that he was not Prime Minister till later. This boat was built on Lifeboat Plain by old Robert Emery, known locally as 'Caller'. They were a wonderful family for boat building and this one was built of oak. It was over 16 feet long on the keel, with copper nails. The bill for this boat states the cost to have been £28 on completion. Well that served my father and his partner, old 'Gayton' Cooper, a cousin of his. The boat *Premier* was the largest boat on the beach and was later sold to a fisherman at Wells who originated at Sheringham, a member of the Cox family who paid £60.

After we had been going to sea together for a few years, the First World War started and nearly all of the fishermen were called up into the trawler section of the Royal Navy. I was one of the first to receive my papers and I had to report to Chatham with many others. I managed to pass the medical tests here in Sheringham, but was only kept at Chatham for about three days. During that time I had to take several medical tests and was told I was not fit enough for service, but to go home and support the country with helping to supply food. Also I had to join the fishing reserves which meant possible call-up to serve on board trawlers out of Hull or Grimsby. As it turned out I never did have to go and, being a member of the lifeboat crew, the remainder of the First World War was spent being called out many times to ships in distress. As I loved serving in the lifeboat I did not miss many times of service.

At the end of the war, Sheringham fishermen were finding it more profitable to fish off the Lincolnshire coast. They were being paid eight or nine shillings a score for crabs, where at home we were only getting two shillings and sixpence, so this made us decide to join them. We went as far as Withensea off the Yorkshire coast. We spent sixteen to eighteen weeks staying in Grimsby and Cleethorpes; many relatives of the Sheringham men lived there so we felt quite at home. We earned far better money and many of the men decided to get their wives and families to join them. There are still descendants of those families at Grimsby and Cleethorpes today. I hoped my wife would do the same, but she didn't do so and after some months of fishing we returned to Sheringham.

Our boat at this time was the *Little May* built in 1921 at Sheringham. She was a whelk boat and weighed three tons and was a very good boat for getting us to the whelk grounds. My partners were Fred 'Dingy' Middleton and Jimmy 'Mace' Johnson. We worked well together. There were quite a few whelk boats at that time, the *Liberty*, owned by the Billy 'Cutty' Craske family and the *Dorothy, Colley, Fern* and the *Girl Gladys*. They were very long and hard days, from early morning to the end of the day. Steaming out to the whelk grounds would take many hours as they were about three to four miles off. We would be gone most of the day, hauling and baiting the pots, returning with our catches and preparing the boats for the next day's departure.

Baiting the lines, East Promenade, c.1927
L to R: Bob, 'Stilly' Little, Father and 'Tooshy'.

9.   Lifeboat Days of World War I

(Father's story continued)

In those far off days when I was a young man, we were all crazy to get into the lifeboat - some even got to fighting to see who would get a jacket first. You see, we had to run a mile and a quarter to reach the lifeboat shed over the golf links.This housed the *J.C.Madge* which arrived, about 1904. She was the lifeboat which came after the *William Bennet.*

I loved the lifeboat service and served in the boats every chance I got.There were many rough times when we had to go to the assistance of some poor fellows; some crews we had to take off before their ships sank. In those days of the Great War, it wasn't a bed of roses!

Now that I am writing about the lifeboat service, I must mention that my whole family before me were lifeboat men. My grandfather on my mother's side of the family was coxswain of the first R.N.L.I. boat that came to Sheringham, the *Duncan,* and I think he held that position for nine years; in fact, when it got time for him to make way for another coxswain he was none too pleased and the committee had some problems getting him to relinquish the job. But I will tell you all about 'Old Philloo' later on. At one time there was a photograph of him and all the crew going down the slipway out of her shed.

The lifeboat shed in those days was on Lifeboat Plain and the slipway ran down alongside the coal yard, adjoining the Crown pub. This was a real hazardous place for the men to get her down and into the water. Later on the committee agreed to find a better place for launching, as I have said, over the links. This slipway was entirely washed away during a northerly gale in 1897 with cliffs eroded, the pub too and the sea wall gone.

The *William Bennet* was here at that time and she was kept in Beach Road for a long time, never did go back into her shed. The last one to be housed over the golf links was the *J. C. Madge* and then in 1936 a new boat house was built along at the end of the promenade. This made it a great deal better for us when we had to get her.

All of these boats had been rowing and sailing and were open to all weathers. Often we were wet through by the time we launched as great sheets of icy water would come right over the sides. All the same, it didn't stop us racing to get in them. It meant a part in trying to save a life and also some well-earned money, but most of all it was the love of it.

I served in the *Henry Ramey* as well. She was the private boat given to the fishermen by the Upcher family because so many lives were at risk when the fishermen were off at sea. This boat was often launched when there was any immediate danger, rather than running all the way over the links, being housed at the top of the West End gangway. There had to be plenty of men to get her down and to re-house her because we didn't have any mechanical aids. There was a crew of sixteen, and sometimes double that number when the weather was bad, to be on the oars to pull her through the breakers.But of course, there were a lot of men around in those days, mostly fishermen or working on the beach, who would all give a hand.

Then the *Manchester Unity of Oddfellows* came. She was a brand new boat, one of the latest types of motor boat and was paid for by the members of the Manchester Unity of Oddfellows Society. A strange thing happened the last year I was at sea. They had to launch the lifeboat for me and my chum as the weather had suddenly deteriorated and the sea become rough. Here was I at sea, waiting for the lifeboat, given by the Oddfellows, coming to the aid of an old Oddfellow like me. I had been a member of the Society since a young lad. Most fishermen of the town were Oddfellows in those days.

I believe I've told you before that in my young days I was eager to get in the boat. On one occasion, I was able to get a jacket but was told I was too young and had to take it off much to my disappointment. I was then 17 years and 9 months old. I had to hand the jacket over to someone else standing near me. About two years later the same thing happened with another of my chums and he wrote to the Institution about it, so when the Inspector visited our station, he proceeded to go over to the notice board and read what it said. With that, he tore the notice off the board. I often laughed about it but was thankful I spent all my years serving in the boats to the best of my ability. Even after I had three serious operations in the Norwich Hospital, I still managed to get along to the boathouse to help her off. I was then 65 years old, but as I neared 70 the coxswain told me the Institution had made a rule that anyone of 70 years was not allowed to go down anymore. Some little distance further along the coast, there had been an accident with some of the older helpers and it was felt advisable to stop the older ones going. I had served in her until I was 60 and a helper until I was 75, so I had to be content, but as the sea and the lifeboat and all it entailed had meant so much to me, it was hard not to be part of it all and go to the boathouse when the maroons were fired. I slowly realised that now I must listen to all those telling their yarns about the rescues they had been to.

One of the first rescues I took part in was to the barge the *Lord Morton*. This was just before the first World War, November 24th, 1909. Everyone had assembled on the cliff to see what was happening when a vessel was seen in difficulties. Both the *Henry Ramey Upcher* and the *J. C. Madge* were launched and those of us in the *Madge* were able to get to her first. Her steering gear was disabled and she asked us to stand by in case we were needed. We finally got her in tow and proceeded towards Yarmouth. Our coxswain that day was 'Click' Bishop. We launched to the rescue of the *Lord Morton* on the Wednesday afternoon. The barge had had a punishing time in the very bad weather we had just had, and the three men had been showing flares and burning everything they could as they had drifted southwards, attempting to alert the coastguard from Brancaster onwards. It wasn't until they were off Sheringham that help was forthcoming. Some of our crew managed to get aboard her and rigged up her steering gear. The men, I remember, were totally exhausted, worn out with battling in such weather. Their boat was completely un-manageable; they had burnt every drop of oil they possessed in an attempt at being rescued. We got to Yarmouth on the Thursday morning!

One of the worst rescues I ever had to go to, was one dreadfully cold night in February, 1916. It had been snowing off and on nearly all day. Halfway through the evening, we heard the rockets to summon the crew of the lifeboat. It was a dreadfully dark night and when we struggled across the links, the bunkers were full of snow. A lot of us blundered into them in our haste to get there. I well remember the soldiers with their bayonets shouting 'Halt; who goes there'. You must remember we didn't have any lights over the golf course - it was as black as ink, apart from the white snow and driving blizzard blowing a hard gale from the north east. As soon as we got to the Old Hythe, the men were scrambling to get their jackets and old Obadiah Cooper, who was then the coxswain cautioned us all with these words 'Well boys, we've got a job tonight. There's no other boat can get off and it's up to you all. If you want to go, then get into the boat'. We all scrambled aboard, never realizing what we were letting ourselves in for. The coxswain

J.C.Madge at the Old Hythe. Standing in the boat: Jim 'Mace' Johnson and 'Old Potter' Hardingham. Father is the first man seated on the left.

took no fewer than thirty men to bank the oars because the sea was so bad. We managed to get her out of the breakers and by this time, there weren't many of us who had any dry clothing on. This was the rescue of the S.S. *Ulla* and it was the Thursday night when we launched the *J. C. Madge*. The steamship had been in some difficulties for a couple of days and had sent up distress flares. When we got to her off Blakeney, the Captain told us he had been on a sandbank and had 5 ft of water in her forehold, but he thought he would try to reach port if we would stand by him. The vessel was in a bad way and looked as if she was going to sink any minute. They were making water fast and it seemed as if with all pumps going, they were all going to be lucky to keep her afloat. At daybreak they got the anchors up and a start was made for the Humber. We then acted as Pilot for the vessel with the hope of keeping her afloat. The *Ulla* was a Norwegian ship, loaded with a cargo of coal and with the amount of danger she had been in, hitting sands two if not three times, and then drifting nearly ashore, none of us felt it was going to be possible. But somehow we did get her into the Humber. I don't think I ever felt so cold in my life. Most of the time the wind had been blowing hard from the East and we could hardly hang on to the oars - we seemed frozen to them. By this time it was the Saturday and we had been gone from Sheringham for three days, our wives and mothers, families and all, thinking that we had been sunk by a submarine, or lost. No news had got through to all our relatives because lines of communication were down owing to the severe gales. Luckily for all of us who were in our boat, we were well looked after by all the folks at Grimsby - they couldn't have done more for us. We were all hungry and frozen with cold but soon recovered. Then we made our way back home on the Sunday morning. A French steamer had us in tow; this was a great help but it was a dirty trip home with snow squalls and a head wind. All the folks at home were waiting for us; they lined the cliff edge and cheered us as we got in.

49

My wife was glad to see me; we had two young ones at that time and they were anxious days. She said 'We thought you had been sunk with a mine or something!'

Another one was the *Alice Taylor* on 18th April, 1917. That was a nasty one but thankfully we were able to get all the crew off her before she sank. There were 18 of them and we were able to get them into Yarmouth. We stayed alongside her as long as we could. It was after midnight. Then all of a sudden her bulkhead gave way and she went down in five minutes. She had previously hit a submerged wreck and had holed herself very badly, but she still had steam and had wanted to try to reach Yarmouth. As I say, we had kept alongside her; it was a very rough night; snowing and blowing almost a gale. Well, all had gone fairly well when we were just off Winterton. Then suddenly, she fired a big red flare. We rushed up alongside and the crew decided to jump into the lifeboat. They were lucky as the sea was running high. One chap had jumped but fell between the boats. The lifeboat crew were able to get him when he came up to the surface. As soon as it became daylight, we made our way but we weren't allowed to go through the Cockle Gate till it got light.

Eventually, all of the crew of the *Alice Taylor* were taken to the Sailors Home, but unfortunately for us, they told us they couldn't do anything for us. So there we were, cold and hungry. We kept walking about all day and we had nothing to eat until a policeman saw us in the Market Place and after he had heard our tale, he took us all along to the Town Hall. There they kindly told us where we could go and get a good meal, and we were very glad to do this, but everything put in front of us was stone cold! Mind you, we were hungry enough to eat anything. But the policeman hadn't forgotten us for he saw to it that we got a really hot meal later on.

Then of course, there was the problem of where we should lay our heads that night. After a little discussion, we were taken to a Seaman's Chapel where we slept on the floor - I think it is where the Scotch girls had been leaving their gear, and also sleeping. Anyway, it was a lot better than another night in an open boat.

What a difference today - a much better boat, every modern convenience, warm clothing and everything available for when they get to a harbour. No rowing or sailing, but the best that money can buy - as it should be for those who risk their lives at sea.

There have been a lot of wrecks in my time. I have seen all kinds of ships, some large, some small. Quite a number have been laden with coal, some with wood. Some have been at the top of high water mark, high and dry, and we have been able to get bags of coal from them. I remember one such ship during the 1914 War. She got ashore near Cley. She had run into some minesweepers and had got a large hole in her. She was bound for Italy with about 4,000 tons of coal in her. The captain had had to beach her and we were told that we could go and fetch what coal we could carry and pay two shillings for it. We had a real good time at this, as it lasted for a week or more. Several of the Sheringham fishing boats were glad to take advantage of this and went back and forth to where she lay, some even suggested going on Sunday but I thought 'No, we've got plenty of other days'.

One very great tragedy I can recall was just before the outbreak of World War One. This was the loss of the S.S. *Heathfield* from Glasgow. It started on a very cold night, blowing about a force 8 with squalls of rain and sleet, but the coastguards of Sheringham and Cromer reported that she was not flying a distress signal and they presumed she was at anchor. That Wednesday night, as I say, there was a terrific north-easterly gale and it did not abate all next day. On the Thursday, the coastguards sighted her off Blakeney or Cley about eleven o'clock in the morning. The lookout kept a sharp eye on her. Of course the weather was very bad and every time we looked at her through the glasses, she looked the same, but she could only be seen between the squalls of rain. She was in the same shipping lanes as several Scottish herring boats and had been passed by, very closely, by some of them on their way to the fishing grounds.

Just after two o'clock in the afternoon, when the coastguards looked again through their glasses, they could see nothing at all. It seemed a complete mystery. Therefore, no attempt had been made to launch either the Cromer or Sheringham lifeboats at that time. Then a message was received that she was flying a distress signal from about five miles out. The lifeboat crew quickly mustered, but by this time deemed it impossible to launch the boat. Blakeney was then communicated with, as here they thought the conditions were a lot better. We heard later she had foundered on Sheringham Shoal. The tragedy was that two of her crew managed to get ashore near Cley and their story was that she had sunk about a half an hour after they left her. For many days there was hope that the men had been picked up by a passing vessel, but most of the bodies were washed up on to the Lincolnshire coast - 16 poor chaps. We were all very upset about this and we later heard that an enquiry was held at Glasgow to find out why the lifeboats weren't launched. The coastguards of Cromer had to attend, also the coxswains of the lifeboats and the two men who had been saved. It seemed that she had got on to a sandbank off Sheringham suffering a great deal of damage, and had sunk very quickly. There was a lot of talk later on about what should have been done and wasn't. A very grievous and sad job and one in which anyone involved had a lot of regrets. The papers said she had struck Sheringham Shoal at 9.30 that Thursday morning and was there three hours before foundering.

Another one I recall is the *George Royle* which was lost on January 23rd 1915. She was lost with all hands, and the Dudgeon Light vessel *Empress* - all hands lost. It was in the early part of the First World War when the *George Royle* was lost. No-one knew what had actually happened to her. She had either struck a mine or had hit the Racebank. Her owners were very keen to reach her as she was fully insured, but the saddest thing to see was on the following morning. There were about twenty or more poor fellows washing about in the low tide, about one mile or so west of Sheringham. I didn't go that way but heard that the water was full of dead bodies. It appeared that the chaps had been trying to make the shore in one of their boats when it reached the large breakers off shore. It must have capsized and they didn't stand a chance in the surf and heavy swell. Her crew were mainly from the South Shields and Newcastle area. The Captain T. Raine was amongst those lost. Later on we heard some of the poor chaps had been buried at Upper Sheringham, but some were taken to their homes for burial at the last moment.

A few days after this, I happened to be walking through Upper Town when I met some of the local chaps, Stephen Purdy and Bob Laxen, with a few others. They began talking about the incident and wanted to know what had happened as they had sighted big red flares coming from the direction of the Old Hythe far to the North. 'Joyful' they said 'whatever was it the other night; the whole sky was alight with these here flares'. Well, then I told them what had happened.

Now I wasn't very eager to pick up a dead body on the beach, so I didn't go asking for trouble if I could help it. I decided to keep east of the town if I was going to go along the beach at all. My wife said to me 'Willie, I wouldn't go along there, if I was you. You might walk upon one of those poor chaps and you'd never forget it'. So I kept this in mind, but all the same, I couldn't keep away from the beach for long and decided to have a walk in the other direction, towards Cromer. As I went along the promenade, I happened upon old Mr Brownsell, who was sweeping the prom. This was his job, so we stopped and had a chat. After we had passed the time of day he said 'Well, Henry Willie, I suppose you're going to have a walk along the beach' and I remarked 'Yes, if I can get round Marle Point' as the seas were washing right up to the foot of the cliffs and it looked a bit difficult to dodge the waves - you had to judge a good time to chance it. 'Well' he said 'watch your chance and make a run for it. 'Yes old partner I'll watch it' I replied. Then I left him and wandered further along. As I say, the sea was still very rough with a strong breeze and I had to wait some time before I could see my chance. When it did come and the sea had flowed back a little, I made a quick dash, stumbling along the beach to escape the next breakers rushing up the beach. Almost at a run and a jump over the little breakwater I found myself almost on top of a poor young fellow, washed up by the tide. He hadn't got

Father, Henry William West

a stitch of clothing on him, just a belt round his waist. The sight of the poor chap made me make a hasty retreat, not even watching out for the tide. I got back up on to the promenade far quicker than I had gone along it. I can see it now as clearly as all those years ago.

Waiting there on the prom was old Brownsell, leaning on his broom and these were his words to me 'I thought you would get him right enough, I had just seen him go over the breakwater when you came along, and you know you will have to go and report the body and where you found it.' I stood looking at him, sort of thunderstruck and still feeling a bit upset. He went on 'Yes, you know you'll have to help get him to the mortuary and then you'll get the 5/- which will be due to you' As he was saying all this, my mind was thinking there was no way out. I would have to go through all this and I wasn't looking forward to it at all, but out of the corner of my eye, I could see he was trying to weigh me up and he had a sly look on his face. Suddenly he said ' 'Course you know, I could do all that for you if you like. Report it and then I would be entitled to the 5/-.' The money didn't trouble me a bit - he seemed eager to do it and that let me out.

That same night we got our first visit from the Zeppelins and they dropped a bomb in the little house in the far corner of Whitehall Yard where 'Bunker' Bob lived. The bomb came right through the ceiling of the bedroom where his daughter was in bed. Luckily it didn't explode and soldiers ran into the house and managed to put it into a pail of water. That same raid, they dropped a few fire bombs in the road where we lived.

One rather amusing incident happened, that I must tell you about. One Saturday night, we were called out to the aid of two French boats. Both of them had been towed from the north by a tug. They were loaded with coal, even their decks were full of coal, but the

French crew had got into the tug. Anyway, we went and had a good look at the two vessels and we decided that probably the inside boat was worth saving. Later on that same Saturday night, my two partners said to me 'Go and see old 'Mace' and hear if he would be ready to go with us and get the *Madeline* off.' Well, when I knocked at his door, his wife said 'He's only just gone to bed, but shout up the stairs and hear what he says'. So I shouted 'Jimmy, are you willing to have a go to see if we can get the *Madeline* off?' With that, the reply was 'I don't think it's much b--- good going after her.' Whereupon, I shouted goodnight to him and then went off to tell the others. With that, we made our way homewards to bed. But on the Sunday, I generally had to have a look at the sea and probably have my glass of beer. When I got to the cliff, I was absolutely thunderstruck. There were ten or a dozen fishermen carrying up sails, ropes, coal, boxes and anything they felt was worth saving. They had been making good progress whilst we had slept. My chums weren't very pleased about this and swore about Jimmy. In fact, I daren't repeat the words they used! One of them said to me 'I bet you'll find that this afternoon all that lot (meaning the other fishermen) will go back and see if they can get one of the boats afloat.' His words proved right, for that afternoon they went back to Blakeney to see if they could salvage one of the fishing vessels. When they got on board, they decided to locate where the water was coming in, then repair it if possible and refloat her. Just at that moment, one of the chaps lit a match - the next there was a terrific explosion. One man was badly burned and most of them had their beards and whiskers singed. They looked a rum old lot when they got back, and those of us who had stayed behind had the last laugh after all.

A few weeks after this incident, the lifeboat was called out as word had been received from Cley coastguards that a small craft was aground on Blakeney Point. The sea had been extremely rough but was improving every hour, so we were able to launch and get alongside the vessel. After hailing her and getting as close as we could, we found no one on board. What had become of them, no one knew. Later, it was discovered that one of the survivors had got ashore and had walked over the marshes to Blakeney watch house. He was in a state of utter exhaustion and on the point of collapse. He was ill for a long time after that, so we were told. He did make a statement that there were 8 in the crew. She was a Norwegian boat and when the crew had got into the breakers, they had all been lost, trying to get to the shore. If they had only stayed in the boat, they would have been saved. Blakeney Point is a dreadful place for anyone to find themselves on. One can easily get drowned on the marshes. The remains of this ship still lie there today, or did when I was at sea. Sometimes she would be completely covered with sand. Her mast stood up for, I should say, 16 years or so and when we were whelking down at Blakeney, we would often use that as a landmark and with another object on shore, we would use this as a guide to our pots; it would take us on to a good area for whelks and the whelk grounds.

Sometime after this, there was another Norwegian boat, but I can't remember her name. She was lost with all hands about three miles south-east of Cromer. I did hear the fishermen of Overstrand say that they had heard the poor fellows calling out for help - of course, in the early days there was no wireless, as we have today. Hardly a week went by without some ship would be in distress.

Another one to strike a mine was the *Rose Lea* of Penarth. She was a brand new ship on her maiden voyage for the United States, loaded with corn. The lifeboat went off to her as soon as she was seen to be in distress. When we got alongside, her master told us he was for running her ashore. We then told the chap it was a nice soft bottom as where this had occurred was off Weybourne. We all thought this was what he would decide to do, but as it turned out, he must have decided otherwise. So we ran two anchors out for him, one weighing about a ton, the other one smaller. For the following three weeks, the weather held fine but nothing ever came to get her afloat again, or came near her, so she was left and her remains are there to this day.

Now, I would like to tell you a yarn about the great steamer which got into difficulties during a very rough gale, blowing hard from the north east. The vessel was having great difficulty in holding her head to the wind and was drifting slowly ashore. After a while, the master decided to lower his anchor to see if that would hold her, but it did not make a great deal of difference - she was still being blown ashore. So he pulled up the distress flags for assistance. The ship was then right off Cromer. The maroons were fired and the *Louisa Hartwell* was launched into a heavy sea. She made a good launch but the seas were so great she was unable to get through the terrific breakers and she began to drift towards Windham Park, west of Cromer. Now she was able to proceed towards the stricken ship and was able to get several of the crew.

Quite a number of her crew had launched their own boat, trying to make for the shore by themselves, but they capsized in the surf, being flung into the sea. This happened during the 1914-18 War and many soldiers, billeted in the district, had lined the cliffs with civilian spectators. They immediately formed a human chain in the icy water and were able to reach the men struggling there. Many of the soldiers were ill for sometime and a few were taken to Cromer Hospital.

On that same day, whilst we here in Sheringham were keeping a watch on things, a number of us stood on the sea wall looking out for ships that might be in distress. We had a good pair of binoculars and I looked. Suddenly, I saw a ship and at that moment whilst I was looking at her, I saw her funnel go down and then everyone had a good look through the glasses. They all said the same 'She look as if she has hit a mine or been torpedoed'. About an hour after this, we heard she was aground, south-east of Cromer, fairly close in with waves breaking over her. It seemed as if it was going to be a real job to reach her and get the fellows off. With the strong gale-force winds and tremendous seas, the *Louisa Hartwell* was again launched, but could not get through the surf. She was washed ashore again and again. They tried to get her through the breakers; darkness was coming on now and our lifeboat secretary then decided twelve of us should go to Cromer to see if we could be of assistance to the Cromer men. So we were driven to Cromer and we helped them to get the *Louisa Hartwell* on to the carriage again. This was achieved about a couple of times as the weather was so bad. The Cromer men were almost exhausted by the events of the day and night; each time they tried to get within a short distance of her, they nearly capsized. When the divisional officer heard that Sheringham men were in the town, he came over to us and asked us if we would give the Cromer men a rest, as they were worn out with all the day's work. We readily agreed to this and said we would be only too pleased to help in any way we could. We offered to get into the lifeboat and do our best under the circumstances.

But Coxswain Blogg consulted amongst his men and it was decided they were still going to reach the ship. She was called the S.S. *Fernebo* and fortunately they were able to reach her and save all the men, except the engineer. He had been badly injured in the explosion and was later picked up the following day, on the beach at Overstrand. He had been in the other part of the wreck which came ashore opposite the lighthouse.

10. *World War II Lifeboat Days*

(Father's story continued)

When the War broke out in September 1939, the *Foresters Centenary* was here then and was often called off to the airmen or planes which came down. Most of the young men of the town had been called up into the Royal Navy for minesweeping or on boom defence vessels. The town was full of military and these often came to the boat house to help us get her off. They didn't fire the maroons but we got summoned by a 'call up' who would come and give us a loud knock, day or night. One such time was on 6th December, 1939 at the very beginning of the War. It was a nasty night with hail storms and driving rain. Suddenly there was a shout at the front of the cottage and some large bangs. Before this, although we were all in bed, it must have been about one o'clock, we had all heard sounds of a low-flying aircraft making a hell of a racket, spluttering and back firing, or so it seemed.

My daughter heard Mr 'Downtide' shout 'It's the lifeboat' so she came to my room and said 'Dad, they're going to launch'. I got into my clothes and began running to the seafront. It was pitch black and blowing hard from the north east. We had to grope our way along the prom. Near the whelk coppers, we saw a large parachute draped on the promenade - everywhere a stench of petrol. I was a bit anxious because my daughter would go with me. When we got to the lifeboat shed, quite a lot had gathered on the breakers' edge. There was a heavy swell in the water and washing on to the stones. Near the break-water, there was a twin-engined plane. At first we thought it was one of ours, but hanging in the cockpit were some binoculars and we realised it was a Nazi bomber. Some of the fellows had got ropes fastened to her and the breakwater to hold her fast. The lifeboat was launched into the darkness to search for survivors, but it was two or three days before the German airmen's bodies were washed ashore. They were buried in the cemetery, in Weybourne Road.

The strange thing about all this is, we could have stripped her clean. Her engines had come out of her and are still there off the lifeboat house today. But when daylight arrived, the town and promenade, beaches, everywhere, was manned by the military. They were stopping everyone from getting within yards of her, saying she was brought down by a secret weapon near Beckham. There were many rumours of lights on her as she came over the links. The town was buzzing with every conceivable rumour. The London papers were full of it. Actually, I believe she was mine-laying and had probably been hit by guns.

As the war progressed, the fishermen spent all their time at the boathouse, ready for an immediate launch. She was always prepared for a quick get-away and we took our gear there to mend, so we could get into her if needed The beaches were out of bounds and there were barbed wire entanglements to prevent an enemy landing. We were able to get to our boats, but we had to have passes and a permit to get petrol for our motor boats. The cliffs each side of the town were mined and several tank traps lay at approaches to the beach. The military were everywhere. The golf links were out of bounds and there were hundreds of soldiers installed here. They had underground bunkers and roads, all named, - a complete military establishment! On the top of Skelding Hill were 3 or 4 naval guns, built into the cliff edge, but later these same guns, when fired, caused the cliffs to subside and it was felt that the cliffs would not be firm enough to hold them although they had been concreted in with brick foundations, so these guns were not used. We had Weybourne Camp to our left and Beeston Hill was also out of bounds with guns and artillery, troops and WAAFS. All of Beeston Hill was barbed wired and also had several gun emplacements.

I must tell you one very funny thing about the War. A Mr D. owned Weybourne Mill. I think he was the first to modernise it and make it into a lovely home. He regularly went fishing with me and my son or with my old chum 'Fatty' Pegg and we sometimes took his daughter,Diana. He would call and say 'Are we going fishing today, Faithfull?' My nickname is 'Joyful' but he always called me 'Faithfull' but I didn't mind. He loved getting off to sea, 'railing' or 'kipping'. In the early part of the War, he called one day to tell us that there was a lot of wood being washed ashore near the lane leading down to the sea from the mill. It had been very rough and for days there had been a strong northerly wind, so he invited me and my daughter over to collect this wood and bring it back in a trailer. My future son-in-law was on leave at that time-just home from Scapa Flow and he came too.

We went and had a look at the debris washing ashore. Amongst it were some bodies, so my daughter made a hasty retreat back to the windmill. Later on after we had seen the military and told them, we were shown all over the windmill. It was handsomely done and one could see for miles, a real landmark from the air and sea. When we were right at the very top of the mill, he said jokingly, 'There you are "Faithful", look out there, I can keep my eye on you when you're getting the short lobsters out of your pots!'. Then we sat down to afternoon tea, sitting at a long dining table. Mrs D. sat at one end and Mr D. at the other with my daughter and her young man at one side and me on the other - we seemed miles apart. There was honey and bread and butter and cakes for tea, and on the far wall was a large map of the east coast and North Sea. I was of course quite used to Mr D., but had not met his wife before. She was very friendly and talkative with a foreign accent, sounding to us German or Austrian. My future son-in-law was wearing his naval uniform and she became eager to ask him about Scapa Flow. Just a few weeks before this, had been the tragic sinking of the *Royal Oak* at Scapa by a U-boat. Billy chatted away happily about the Navy and Scapa Flow, every now and then getting a nudge under the table from my daughter. Well we had an enjoyable time and then we went home. When we got indoors Bill suddenly said 'Why did you keep kicking me?' 'Well you were very forth-coming about Scapa Flow, weren't you? I wish you had been more careful.' He just laughed.

Several months later 'Fatty' came to see me. 'Hev you heard about Mr D. I hear that they have locked him up. Seems that they were spies!' Then he told us all the yarns he had heard. The village folk at Weybourne felt the windmill should be camouflaged and had been to see him, but he had refused and rumours had got around of other incidents. Well, to say the least, I was right thunderstruck at all this news, and everywhere I went and met anyone that knew him, they would all say 'What's all this about Mr D., is it right?' Well you know how things get exaggerated, so I felt I was going to take it all with a pinch of salt. Whenever the gentleman had come to see either Fatty or me, he was generosity itself. He came perhaps with eggs or butter or ham. Perhaps at Christmas time a bottle of wine - I really could hardly believe all the gossip which was going around.

The months passed on and none of us saw him and we assumed it must be true. Then just before the 'doodlebugs' started to hit the south east, a knock came on the door one day and there he was. 'Hello, Faithful' he said, 'just brought you a few things. I have been to see poor Fatty and what's all this I hear - you've all thought I was held by the police for consorting with the enemy?' I didn't know what to say at first, but agreed there had been a

Low water, getting the boats down. L to R: Father, Arthur Cox, Jim Bishop in distance, Bill Ayers (the author's husband) on leave, and Uncle Bob 'Joyful'.

rare lot of rumours although it was very nice to see him again. He then made the remark that the family were leaving Norfolk and going to live in Kent, so it was the last time I saw him. We later heard that he had been killed in one of the doodlebug raids, and his only son was taken captive by the Japanese - they owned tea plantations out there.

During the first part of the Second World War, the convoys came in very close to Sheringham. Crowds of people would line the sea wall and watch the enemy planes as they circled and dive-bombed the lengthy convoys. All were escorted by several destroyers. It was quite horrific to see all of this, they were so close in. Later mine-fields were laid and the convoys went further out. Like a lot of the other fishing families, we owned a marine band radio and we would tune it to the lightships. This was another horrendous occupation, for we could hear quite plainly when they were calling for assistance, the lifeboats too, saying they were being machine-gunned. One such occasion was when the *East Dudgeon* was bombed. The lifeboat was launched to search for survivors. It was a bitterly cold day - I think this was in 1940-41. When the lifeboat returned, the crew members said they hadn't found anyone on board but the lightship had received a lot of damage, so had evidently been attacked. It was hoped that all the crew had been picked up by another ship - they had searched for several miles in icy conditions, but found nothing.

The following day, in a bitterly cold wind, the lifeboat was launched and searched to the west of the town. They had been asked to do this by the secretary as no news had been heard of the missing men. It was felt that if they had been picked up, information would have been received by the coastguards. The lifeboat was finally recalled when news was received that the lightship's crew had been washed up on the Lincolnshire coast. There was one survivor who told his story. The lightvessel had no radio and couldn't transmit, so no one knew who had sent the message that they were being bombed and machine-gunned. Could it have been the German plane? No one ever did know who it was.

All sorts of things washed ashore. Once there was a lot of oranges. They were scattered all along the beach at high water mark. It wasn't long before crowds were there picking them up. One rather mysterious lot of objects came in all along the beach. This was in the earlier days of the War. Long tubular black rubber-like material, filled with something; we couldn't make head nor tail of that. Quite a few of us took the lengths home to see if any use could be made of it. When it was split open with a sharp knife, the creamy like material inside proved to be hard packed kapok and once pulled out of its casing was used to fill cushions. My wife and daughter decided to make a couple of eiderdowns. They both worked diligently at this but kept complaining of the stuff getting up their noses. It was a bit comical when I got in one day-there they were with masks over their mouths and noses!

Not long after that, I had a walk along the beach one day, and saw some boxes floating in on the tide. Waiting until some came within reach, I found they were boxes of fat or margarine but covered here and there with shingle. At first I thought they wouldn't be any good but managed to get a couple of boxes home. My wife had a good look at it and decided it was probably lard. The shingle had only managed to get into the cracks in the boxes and we cut off all we could. She then melted down the rest in saucepans and large containers, and strained it all and put it into clean boxes She lined these with greaseproof paper and it was marvellous lard - no trace of salt in it - just the job to last us for many months and years of the war. I was always very partial to my wife's pastry!

Fate often took a hand when we least expected it, as was proved several times when the lifeboat was launched. One spectacular occasion was when the landlord of the Crown pub, Mr Charlie Holsey, was in his bar serving his usual customers. This pub was used by several of the lifeboat crew who often met here for a game of darts or dominoes. I used the little 'Windham' pub for my daily half-pint but as I say the Lobster and Crown were two of the chief pubs where the coxswain, second cox, bowman and mechanics met. It was only sheer good fortune on that day as the landlord was washing up some glasses. He held one up as he wiped it clean and spotted what he thought could be a boat or plane on the sea, quite a way out. When they got their binoculars and telescope out, he was proved to be correct and the lifeboat was launched. Half an hour later, they were able to rescue five Polish airmen, who had been in a dinghy for a couple of days, drifting along the coast. Their plane had crashed in the Wash and the poor fellows had suffered a great deal. At one time they were nearly ashore, as they could hear the surf, but the wind changed direction, blowing them further from land. It was by sheer good fortune that they had been spotted.

Some of the fishermen were required to go and clean the aerodromes and woodland areas. I remember quite a few of us going up to the woods near Pretty Corner. We had to walk there. We took some grub with us and stayed all day, clearing and taking down several trees. Then when the fishing got bad, a few of us were sent to help prepare the aerodromes that were coming into use. We went in lorry loads, 10 or 12 of us, mostly fishermen. This was something new for all of us, but the situation in the country was so bad, everyone was needed to do war work. We all enjoyed it really. Some of us went to Matlaske aerodrome, Stiffkey Camp and Langham. Another chap and I got sent to Langham airfield and I was told to be labourer for two bricklayers and fetch and carry everything they wanted. Well, I suppose I worked too fast for them because all of a sudden they said 'Hold you on, Joyful. Don't you keep getting too much - this will last us till we knock off'. Well, there was I wondering how I could fill my time. I had always been used to work and now I was being told to slow down! I was working too quickly! Lots of the men were spending their time dodging the foreman and getting into some of the little huts playing cards. Well, anyway, it was a change and that's no mistake. We also went on Sundays and got double time. When I was told I had got to report on that Sunday, I turned up. We did about two hours work and then decided to have our grub. Then there came a little rain, so everybody packed up and went to the 'Langham Bell' where we all stopped, until it was time to go home - even the head man. This was a surprise to me and I said to my wife when I got home 'Mary Ann, I aren't very keen on this sort of business, hiding up in the sheds and wasting time like that. I've never been used to it.' It didn't seem right to me when one thought of all the young fellows risking their lives out there wherever they were to win the War and those at home taking it easy and wasting time. Anyway, I had to stay there for another three months and was glad to earn some money until it was Spring again.

One night I remember, when we were all on our way back from the airfield, we were nearly home when someone smelt smoke. The lorry was alight! We all jumped out as quickly as we could and they managed to put the flames out. Another time when I had been at the aerodrome, I had just got indoors and had my dinner. My wife had gone to the pictures and my daughter and I were looking forward to a quiet evening. Suddenly we heard the sound of a plane's engines - she seemed very low and directly overhead. I calmly made the remark 'It's one of ours.' At that very moment, there was a large explosion - the soot came down the chimney, fire and sparks and debris all over the clean linen on the rack and fireguard. The lights went out, the doors flew off and the window came in right on to my little grandson's cradle. He was just three months old. I thought we had been hit. It was the bitterly cold night of 19th January, 1942 and heavy snow and ice was on the ground. We made the little boy a bottle of milk to keep him quiet but I think that there was probably more soot than milk as we couldn't see much by candlelight. About four doors away, four houses had been levelled to the ground and the soldiers and air raid wardens were trying to dig out survivors. This was the raid on Cremer Street, in which four people lost their lives. All of the street and New Road houses were badly damaged and most occupants evacuated. We stayed in ours. My poor wife at the pictures had had a dreadful shock when the alarm sounded. She rushed outside to be told it was Cremer Street.

When the weather got better, I went to see Bob 'Butterballs' Grice to ask him to be my partner that year at sea as my son was away in the Royal Navy. Bob and I got along very well - he was a good partner to have. By this time, most of the young men of the town were away on active service, so it was left to us older ones to carry on.

At that time, the aircraft of the Allies were attacking Germany and raids continued day and night. The American Airforce would go out all day and our planes all night. We would see them come home with only one or two engines still functioning. We kept going to sea as much as we could. The strange thing was how much the fishing had varied. When I remember the 1914-18 war, there was plenty of fish of every kind to be had - cod, plaice, skate and dabs. Whenever the raids were on, we were on standby duty at the lifeboat station. A message would come through from the American bases and the lifeboat was pulled out of her shed, ready for launching. We were ready for a quick launch and when we were baiting our lines, we would take them along to the shed so as to be on hand every moment of the time.

Before I leave my stories of those years, I think I must mention an episode that happened one cold winter's day. As I have already said, when I wasn't at sea or on the beach, I would love to take a walk in the woods with my barrow and get a few pieces of wood which had blown down. If I went in the right hand side of the woods on Upcher's land, I would often ask the Squire if I could get any bits lying around. He always said yes as he knew the fishing families very well. I had sometimes taken my first little grandson with me - he followed me and went with me a lot. He was about two years old or maybe a little older and I would push him home on the barrow-load of wood. He loved it. But that day it was bitterly cold and snowing and I wouldn't take him. I went to my usual spot, just near Butts Lane that led into Upper Town. Here there are a lot of pine trees and fir and they make a good fire. I left my barrow and began walking about the trees when I suddenly heard the sound of a plane and looking around, to my horror I saw and heard this American bomber crashing through the trees. Great lumps of tree were flying in all directions. It was terrifying - I didn't know which way to run or whether it was going to explode and burst into flames or not. The great bomber, it was a Liberator, came down into a bank at the corner of the field, its propellers and engines held in the pine trees. Then there was sudden silence. I had run a little way into the wood but stopped because I felt perhaps they were alive. Yet I hardly dared go back in case she exploded. One of the men had somehow managed to get clear and called to me saying 'She won't explode, we are out of fuel,' so I went to the nose of the plane and shall never forget the sight of all those chaps, trapped and all on top of one another. I managed to get one chap out and laid him on the bank. I gave him a cigarette then tried to get the others. I then saw a chap running across the fields from Upper Sheringham and between us we got some more - three I think - but one was dead. The other two we carried to a safer place and I gave them a cigarette each. Then I put my overcoat over them. It was snowing hard, with a north-east wind. Their injuries seemed pretty bad and they were in great pain. We were told to take them further away from the plane and I did not go back to the aircraft after that. The U.S. Airforce sent cranes and lifting gear to get the wrecked plane out of its crash site. There were American jackets lying about and maps and equipment. They had been to Kiel Canal that day and had suffered damage from flak. They were based at Wendling I think. Out of the ten in the crew, three or four were dead. Ambulances came and the doctors gave them pain-killers and injections. I held the arms of the airmen as they gave them the injections, then I went home to tell my wife and daughter what had happened. It was a rare good job I didn't take my grandson with me that day. Most days I took him with me and plenty of times he was covered with snow from head to foot as he rode home on the barrow.

I never did know who the young man was who came to help me that day, nor have I seen him since, but a few years ago I went into the Windham Arms one lunch time to get my usual half a pint of beer. A Mr Craske came in and said 'Henry Willie, I wish I could have found you yesterday.' When I asked why he said 'Well, some Americans were in the town and asked me if the fisherman was still about - the one who had pulled them out of the bomber which had crashed in the woods. They would have liked to have seen him to thank him but they had to return to Norwich where they were staying'. So I never met them, but did hear that there had only been four survivors. Each year for a long time, somebody would hang a wreath on the trees near the Holway Road where it happened.

So you see, this is quite a different story from my yarns of the sea.

East Prom in war time.
Note the coils of barbed wire.

11. Granny's Stories

(Father's story continued)

Now I must tell you about my Grandmother West. She was the wife of the Joshua Henry who first acquired the nickname of 'Joyful' and she belonged to the Grice family of Sheringham. Her name before marriage was Mary Ann Grice and after moving from Gun Street when my parents married, they lived in a little house in Station Road called Lavender Cottage. I loved going to hear all her yarns of the old days. She became a widow early in life, so she was real glad of my company. She was a good cook and I thought she cooked better than my own mother. I was always with her, slept there too until I went to sea with my father, so it was considered my home. If there was anything happening in the village, such as the visit of a circus or a fair, she would get down from the cupboard an old pot in which she kept a little money and she would put sixpence into my hand and say 'off you go boy'. Then I would run off to my playmates and we would go to the circus or buy some sweets from Old Brightmer's shop adjacent to the house in which Granny lived.

It was warm and cosy in her little kitchen; she had the usual cast iron grate, polished up so you could see your face in it, with all the steel parts shining and the little tap on the right hand side of the fire was where the water was heated. She would fill this area with water from the town reservoir and we would enjoy our supper together. There would be a saucepan or two on the top of the stove and a big black kettle boiling on the hob. Usually it was rabbit cooking in the oven. The rabbits she kept whole after skinning and stuffing them and putting vegetables around. They were very tasty. Sometimes my cousin John would join us in her little parlour and we would be alright for a little while and then perhaps the novelty of having another person there wore off and we would start to squabble. Whenever this happened, she would get down a little plate off the mantleshelf. On this plate was a painting of two little nigger boys fighting and she would point at these and quote,

'Whatever brawls disturb the street, There must be peace at home.
Where sisters and brothers always meet, Quarrels should never come.'

This was printed all around the edge of the little plate. This might make us a bit quiet for a while, but it never stopped us from quarrelling whenever we got together because I felt that I had more right to be at my grandmother's than he did, which of course was not true!

I used to sit for hours listening to what the old lady had to tell me. After she had lost her husband some years before she told me how she had seen written in the family Bible all the names of the descendants of her family. I too was shown this Bible, but where it went to I never knew. The families of the village all had their large Bibles and births, marriages and deaths were recorded in them. Then later on would be the children's names and birthdates and grandchildren's too. It was a wonderful record of ancestors.

The tale she told me was this. Her mother had been the illegitimate daughter of a young woman of Upper Sheringham by the name of Chesney or Chasteney. This young person worked for a gentleman by the name of Cook Flower. He was the lord of the manor at that time and she was housekeeper for him. In due time the child was born, a little girl named Elizabeth. As the child grew up, Mr Cook Flower would stop and speak to her and later he told the mother of the child that he would have her educated or put to a trade when she became old enough. She was put to dress-making in the hope that she would eventually marry and be in better circumstances. Then he saw her one day in Lower Town talking and associating with the lower classes as he called them - she was with a number of fisher lads and lassies. He called her to one side and told her he didn't want to see her with such rough types again as these would be no good for her. He expressly said to her 'Don't go with those low rough men. I want you to remember that'. But she was a strong-minded person and was courted by Henry Luke Grice, fisherman of Lower Town, and eventually married him, producing several

sons and daughters. Some became fishermen, one or two were bakers. They all had nicknames, 'Mans' Grice, 'Baker' Grice, 'Nanny Mink' and 'Lizzie Tom'. I believe there were three sons and three daughters - one of course was my grandmother, Mary Ann. She said that Cook Flower was buried at Gresham and she had been to the funeral. I myself have seen his gravestone near the right hand side of the graveyard.

Strangely, the name Flower was often added to some of the descendants of families connected as a second name, or even once a boat was built called the *Constant Flower*. The 'Joyful' family used this boat although they didn't own it. So now I have written this all down for you to read and make your own judgment.

Some of the stories Grandmother told were of her days at school. She had to attend the Upper Sheringham school. Once one of the teachers hit her across the head with a ruler and cut her head open. When she got home all the sympathy she received from her mother was 'No doubt it's done you good to get a good thrashing'.

As I have already mentioned Grandmother was married to Joshua Henry West and they had three children one of which had died young. Joshua Henry the son was later to be my father and his sister, Elizabeth, married Robert John Long, so the Longs and the Wests were cousins, related to practically all the other village folk. The little house had a front room or parlour. The front door led into the room, then a doorway to the left of that went into another small room with a staircase leading to two bedrooms. From the little kitchen there was a winding narrow staircase, quite dark, and I was very glad for the candlestick to light me to bed. She had a small lean-to building outside where basins and pails of water were kept. This was where we could wash our faces. There was a small wash-house at the end of the garden which held a copper, small grate in one corner and a sink under the window. If you wanted to get up into what they called the chamber, there was a wooden runged ladder in place. The room was large enough for a bed and could be used for sleeping, but we often played there. They also had an adjoining passageway where there was another small store and where all the fishing things could be kept, nets and pots and gear; this little house is still there as I write this in 1971.

One night I said to my grandmother, 'How did Grandfather get the nickname "Joyful"?' 'Well,' she replied, 'they tell me when he was steering the luggers home he was always singing the same chapel song, or hymn - you must realise they were very strong Methodists and took their religion seriously. He would sing this same hymn in chapel on Sundays, and whenever he got the chance, and this was what he sang:

'Oh joyful Canaan land, Sweet spring is coming on,
A few more months of wind and rain, And winter will be gone.'

No doubt the congregation got a bit fed up with this and would remark, 'Here comes old Joyful Canaan. We shall get the same hymn tonight.' They did not possess an organ and he started the hymns. Eventually they shortened his nickname to 'Joyful'.

Grandmother was a member of the top chapel and they had to pay about 4/- a year for their seats in chapel. Once when the superintendent of the Station Road chapel called to collect money for her seat after her husband had died, she said, 'I heard you had a gathering (meaning a collection of money) for widows and old people a few months ago. My poor old man has been gone a long while. I expect you think I was too well off to get any of it, yet you come collecting off me.' After this reprimand she never heard any more about paying for her seat. She was forever singing hymns and she would sit by the dying firelight singing her favourite 'Oh for a closer walk with God'. Sometimes some of her relations would gather together in the front room and hold a prayer meeting. Many of the old folks came and we boys could hear them inside, especially on a summer's night when the cottage doors and windows were open. Some of my chums would come and sit on the little stone wall which bordered her tiny garden. They thought it was a good idea to creep along these walls and listen to all the old folk. If Grandmother caught any of them she would smartly tell them to 'clear off' or she would give them a 'ding of the lugs'.

She told me there was another chapel a bit further down on the right hand side near where we now have our Post Office. It was called a Ranters' Chapel, a largish building, and inside it was a gallery all round where the choir could get up and sing. There was also a small cemetery there and I have heard that Lewis Emery and his wife were buried there. My Grandmother was a regular member here and had her permanent seat. She would recall how, when she was quite young, she would climb up and look in the chapel windows and see all the people singing and praying. They would hold what they called 'Love Feasts' and would get so carried away that some would swoon and fall down on the floor. They would lie for days, as if in a trance; she said 'No one knew what came over them'.

Before she lived in Gun Street, in the early part of her married life, she lived in 'The Wave' near West Cliff and the little house is there today, but mostly used by summer visitors; it is of course far more modern today. Then it was a tiny fisherman's cottage. A lane led down to these cottages, fenced on one side by a small hedge. Today we can see this area as part of the West Promenade with its railings, and to the right of it is the bridge which goes over the West End gangway. But let us have a glimpse of how it was in her day. She said there was the cliff edge and sometimes a goat or two and sheep would be there, nothing but the sandy beach below. One night she had been out somewhere and as she neared her little home she heard such a hollering and chains rattling she was immediately sure she was hearing the 'Tow Rows'. Now you may have heard about the 'Tow Rows'. A ship was supposed to have sunk off Beeston Hill many years ago when all hands were lost including several poor men who were chained below decks. So whenever anyone heard this awful shouting and clanking of chains, they said 'It's the cries of the poor fellows as they drowned'. So Grandmother felt sure she was hearing the 'Tow Rows' and made haste to get inside her cottage and safety. But when she heard some more rattling this seemed to be coming from the cliff edge, so she ventured a bit nearer, climbed up and peered over the hedge. There below her was 'Old Hart's' large horse. It had slipped down the cliff with all its harness still on it, and there were a couple of chaps doing their best to pull the horse up again. She said 'Of course, if I hadn't gone and looked over that furrow bush, I'd have told everybody that I'd heard the 'High Sprites' or 'Tow Rows'.

They were simple souls and believed all sorts of tales. They lived in fear of drowning at sea. Tragedies were happening all the time and they never knew what was to befall their loved ones. My Granny didn't tell me of the time when my father and his partners were rescued by the *Augusta* lifeboat. My own mother said it was shortly after I was born. They had to launch the private boat to help the 'hovellers' (big boats used then). A gale had blown up very quickly and several of these large boats, my father's boat among them, were trying to make the shore. The *Augusta* managed to get all the men although the boats were badly damaged and some lost in the turmoil. My Grandmother in her distress had run on to Beeston Common and they had to go and find her and bring her home. They got her indoors and saw she had torn her clothing to pieces, she had been almost demented.

Grandmother would pull up her old chair near the fire and start to tell of days long ago. Sometimes I think she would do this so I wouldn't go out and she be left alone. But it was so interesting to listen to her. When she started it was the usual 'Well , course, things were different when I was a girl'. She could remember tales of the Press Gangs and how young fisher lads would run into the woods to hide. The procedure of the Press Gangs was to come ashore from the naval boats and take as many men as they could lay their hands on. They would persuade some to join the navy if that was possible. Some they would buy intoxicating drink so the poor fellows were befuddled and didn't know what was happening until they got on board ship. Some of the village lads were artful and if they found themselves aboard ship they would then make out that they were a bit simple-minded. One in particular managed to get out of it all by doing exactly the opposite to what he was told. When told to push, he pulled - they didn't keep him long and were glad to see the back of him. He always laughed about it and over the years got many a free drink from his pals to recount the tale. A message would be sent to all the cottages when news was received in the village that Press Gangs were about, and men would hide anywhere they could. Then someone would get word to them that all was clear again.

Another story recounted by her was of the very many fights that took place between the 'Shannocks' and any foreigner - anyone that lived half a mile away was a foreigner! Many of the fights took place with the Yarmouth men when the Sheringham men were fishing out of Yarmouth for herrings. As was the usual thing, the Sheringham men couldn't get along with the Yarmouth men and they began to argue amongst themselves which ended in a big fight. At the end of one such fight they threw the Yarmouth men into the river. Well, along came the police and arrested four or five of the Sheringham men and put them all in gaol until the next day. They then had to appear in court to explain the cause of the row and what had actually started the fight. They were found guilty and the Shannocks had to pay £30 or go to prison for a month. Well, none of them possessed this amount of money and even if they counted up every penny between them there wasn't enough, so the situation looked bad, and probably they would have to do 'time' in prison. Somehow, word of this 'row' had reached Mr Upcher at Sheringham. He sent the money to secure their release so that they could return home, but he sent word to all those concerned that the next time they were called out in the Upcher lifeboat to any vessel in distress in which they might obtain salvage money, they would have to divide it into two shares for the boat and one share for the crew (instead of the other way around), and that was how it was arranged. This row which I tell you of was always known as the 'Yarmouth Row'.

I think the last time I went in the *Henry Ramey* was when she went to Blakeney one Saturday night and found the *S.S.Urd* abandoned as all the crew had been taken off by the Wells lifeboat the day before; the boat had been left to sink, no doubt thinking she was almost gone away. When we got to her we found the pumps were useless, so we baled the water out with pails. We had left word in Sheringham that, if we had not returned by a certain time, a tug was to be sent for. At last the *George Jewson,* a tug from Yarmouth, arrived and we managed to get her in tow, the *S.S.Urd* eventually being taken to Yarmouth by our lifeboat. The salvage money was finally decided upon; £32 was allocated to the *Henry Ramey* and £16 to the crew. But some time after this when we were fishing out of Grimsby, we had our share of the salvage money sent to us as Sir Henry Upcher would not take any since the Institution boat was used mainly for rescue work.

Grandmother spoke of another argument the Shannocks had with the crew and Captain of a ship that had gone ashore right opposite the Crown Inn pub. This was the steam ship *Amphion*. She was quite high and dry but would not have anything to do with the Sheringham boat. They preferred to put the job to a salvage firm. This upset the Shannocks and they took the matter into their own hands. What do you think they did? When the salvage firm arrived, they found that all the men of the village had dug deep trenches across the beach and caused as much inconvenience as they could!

All these little snatches of stories Granny would keep me enthralled with. Also this one about the huge white stone which lay for many years against an old man's door. During a great storm this huge stone was washed out to sea and could only be seen at very low tide. It was always called the 'Taylor Stone', but I have heard my father say it disappeared and was never seen again. It was thought by the village folk that a ship had smashed it up.

The old lady used to talk a lot about her wedding day. She said it was a great day and a lot of people had been invited to celebrate the marriage. This was to take place at the groom's mother's home. This would have been Joseph West and his wife's cottage. He was called 'Old Joe Fiddle' and liked his bottle of beer. He was a great character and tales of him always went around the village. He could get especially jovial and argumentative if he supped a drink too many, so some of the women of the invited guests thought it was best if he wasn't around to take part after the marriage in church. So it was agreed he should be locked in the village stocks. Four big men then got him to the crossroads at the corner of what is now Station Road. They unscrewed the stocks and sat him down, bolted his feet in place, and thought they would enjoy a peaceful ending to the wedding feast. 'That's alright' they remarked, 'he's good for a few hours - we shan't hear no more from him till daylight' - never realising how strong a man he was! They were happily engaged when there was a lot of shouting and banging at the little cottage door. There lay 'Old Joe Fiddle' with the remains of the stocks still attached to his feet. He had managed to get loose and get back home. Grandmother said 'He had to be a tough old varmit to do that!'

12. Grandfather Philloo

(Father's story continued)

Another old character in my life was my grandfather on my mother's side of the family. He was Robert Cooper and his nickname was 'Philliloo' or 'Philloo'. I remember when very young visiting him in his little cottage being told to say his name. My tongue could never get around all that, so I called him 'Lu-lu' and for a time the folks called me 'Little Lu-lu'. He was a rare old chap, ready for anything. He was a fisherman, poacher and also a handyman for the Upcher family at Upper Town. In his latter days he would walk to the Old House where they lived and help in the gardens and kitchens. What use he was I could never be sure of. I would see him sometimes walking to Upper Town, especially on a Sunday evening. Once I remember standing near the Town Clock on a Sunday evening with a group of other fishermen. We were listening to the Salvation Army band when suddenly one of our group said 'Isn't that your old grandfather going up to the Hall - it's looking like him. Wherever is he going to at this time of the evening?' I caught up to him and said, 'Where ever a you a going orf to at this time o' the night? Thass a gitting dark.' 'Where d'ya think I'm a going' he answered, 'to work o' course.' With that I took hold of his arm and steered him back towards his home. He was getting old and towards the end of his life, so he had begun to wander a bit. When he got to his little cottage in the tiny yard opposite to Lushers Bakery (we knew it then as Chasteneys Yard) I opened the sneck of his cottage door and we went in.

It was dark inside and you could hardly see a thing. He lived alone then, but before that he had lived with his daughter Mary a couple of doors away. In the room was a table and chairs, sofa and all the usual household items. On the table was a candle stuck in a bottle; all the tallow had been flowing down the bottle and in the gloom I could just see the clock. It had only one hand, the small one, and that was pointing to six. I said 'Do you know it's past seven o'clock? How can you tell the time by that clock?' He said, 'That's alright. I can tell the time alright. I thought it was six o'clock in the morning. I wuz then a gorn up to the farm to du my wark.' Poor old chap. I went and got him his allowances just to pacify him. My own father didn't drink at all at the local pubs but he arranged a sum of money to be used for a weekly allowance of beer for him and Philloo knew exactly what this meant alright.

Robert Cooper was the eldest son of Timothy Cooper and Mary. He was born at Easter, April 1819. He was married when he was just 18 years old, possibly to a relative as her name was Sarah Cooper. They had a few years together until her early death at the age of 36 and she was the mother of his first four children. Then after Sarah's death he married Mary Ann Little by whom he had a further nine children, a total of thirteen in all, but like a lot of families then, some never reached maturity.

He was married to Sarah in 1838 on December 26th at Upper Sheringham church and of the four children one, Mary, married the master of a sailing ship which was wrecked on the Goodwins. His name was Kerrison and when Philloo got old he went to live with Mary in the cottage in Chasteneys Yard. His son, Robert Brown Cooper was always known as 'Old Duncan' because of the family association with the first R.N.L.I. boat called *Duncan* which arrived in Sheringham in 1867. My grandfather was coxswain of the *Duncan* for nine or ten years, but I am getting ahead of myself and will tell you about that later on.

After his first wife died, he married his second wife in 1855 and out of the nine children he had by her one, Esther, was a cripple and she lived until she was sixteen years old. Then a fatal accident happened to her. She fell on to an open fire and was burnt to death whilst alone in the little cottage. Another one, William, the youngest, died from brain fever at the age of thirteen years. His other son, John Charles, died young aged 26 and another son, James, was fishing out of the Humber when he was lost overboard and drowned.

So you see he had his sadnesses and trouble, but he always seemed to be cheerful although I think he was an awkward old cuss and if he made his mind up to do anything, he did it without consideration of the consequences. Like the time when he went to sell some of his gear, nets and boat; he was gone for several days and his wife began to worry about whether he was alright. When he did return home his pockets should have been lined with money, instead of which he treated all and sundry and came home with less money than he had gone with and had bought gear that wasn't half as good and a boat that leaked!

Once when he was ill, a few months before he died, I thought I would take him a couple of lobsters for a treat. They were small and only just the length, for as you know they have to be the required length and if not they have to be thrown back into the sea. Well these two lobsters were small and in all probability I should have thrown them back to live a little longer, but no I thought 'Old Grandfather will like them as he's been poorly, they'll help to cheer him up.' I took them home and my wife boiled them and away I went. He had a quick look at them and said, 'Whatever have you got here? I should think you ought to be ashamed. That ent a going to du nobody any good if you all du this - thass the worst thing you could do. That'll soon finish off all the lobsters.' When I put out my hand to pick the lobsters up again, he said, 'Well, I suppose as you brought them, I'll het to eat em.'

He also had an allotment up where is now the Burlington Hotel. There weren't any large houses in this area in my young days. When you left the coastguard houses near the West End and the ones in Victoria Street there was just fields and allotments. People grew vegetables and all manner of stuff was kept here, old boats and some gear. There was a lane through the fields and us boys would love to go and have a look at his strawberry patch. He did grow some rare nice strawberries and we would have to await our opportunity. Once he chased us and he had a temper I can tell you. We daren't go anywhere near him for weeks. The old man went and told my mother that it was me and I got a real good hiding for that, but a few days later he put out a few of his best fruit for me, so all was forgiven.

He used to tell me of how he went to some of the fields to get a few rabbits or a pheasant or two. He would dress himself up in all old clothes so no one would know him and be gone all night. Very often he would make his way to the kitchen up at the 'Old House'. He got on very well with the cook who worked there and she was very fond of him and would often make him a pie or a meat tart. This was after he lost his second wife, Mary Ann, and lived alone. Those days he would go to my mother's and have his tea, but I

*Great-grandfather, Robert 'Philloo' Cooper
also nicknamed 'Anyhow'.*

had to be real careful if I took him a lobster. He always complained and gave me a long lecture on throwing anything back into the sea that wasn't the length, be it a crab or lobster. Of course he was right, as we knew.

The family at the Hall or 'Old House' had been very concerned at the loss of life at sea amongst the local men, several poor fellows being lost and leaving widows and orphans. The Hon. Mrs Upcher had always shown so much sympathy for them. She had had the private lifeboat built in 1838 by Robert Sunman at Upper Sheringham. This was called the *Augusta* after her youngest daughter who had died at an early age. This boat served the town well many years, but now there was a decision made to have a lifeboat station and Institution boat at Sheringham and a lifeboat house was built near the old coal yard adjoining the Crown pub. This land belonged to Mr Upcher and he gave permission for the shed to be built. The cost of this large building, which still stands today, was £251 and it was built by Mr Francis and Lewis Emery. It consisted of lower rooms to house the new boats and a Reading Room or Lecture Room above with a flight of steps leading up to it. This was where the fishermen met and the committee held their meetings. At first it wasn't certain where the lifeboat shed was to be built. Two sites were chosen, one on the West Cliff and the other on the East Cliff. When it was finally put to the men who would man the new boat, they all agreed that both sites were the same and in the end the site near the Crown Inn was chosen.

When the *Duncan*, the first R.N.L.I. boat, arrived at Sheringham in 1867, my grandfather was then about 48 years old and had served many years in the *Augusta*. He became coxswain of the *Duncan* in January 1876. Each year the men would assemble in the Reading Room to elect a new coxswain and it was with unanimous agreement that he was chosen with Harry West as his assistant. He kept his post up until 1882, but when he was sixty years old the Institute required coxswains to retire at that age. Previously the committee, under instructions from the inspectors, had also informed the fishermen that a permanent coxswain was to be appointed instead of an annual one and that he too would have to retire at sixty years of age.

Now 'Philloo' wasn't too happy to retire. When the time came, he didn't turn up for several meetings of the committee and neither did some of the other fishermen. From all accounts the secretary had a rare old job to get Robert Cooper to see reason. He had been voted in each year by all of the fishermen, and when finally he was told in the April of his 61st birthday that he was expected to retire, he had reluctantly to agree, but it caused a lot of trouble at the time.

He got a few reprimands in his time, one of which was about the time he was due to retire. This was when a brig was sighted labouring heavily in a gale. She was flying a distress signal, but as she was nearer to Cromer than Sheringham, the lifeboat did not go to her assistance. Philloo was called before the secretary and reprimanded. Whilst this was going on the vessel became a wreck near Cromer, but the Cromer lifeboat did not launch, so at last the *Duncan* went to its assistance hurriedly taken by road, pulled by horses and carriage, but found the seas too rough to launch at Runton. The ship was now a complete wreck and the men were clinging to part of the ship nearer the shore. The Sheringham fishermen waded into the heavy surf and saved four of the crew.

Another memorable occasion much talked about was the launch of the *Duncan* to a Norwegian barque, the *Carolina*. This occurred on the 6th of December, 1882, and when the ship was sighted it was flying a distress signal. Also watching this vessel were the men who usually manned the *Augusta,* just a few yards further along to the westwards on the cliff. They too were eager to launch their boat. You must realise there was a bit of rivalry between these two boats and they were eager to get the prize. It was always a race to see who would launch first. This time it happened to be the *Augusta* boatcrew who were able to get to the ship first. They managed to rescue all of the men and brought them safely ashore. As you know this wasn't a very good occasion for the Institution boat, for although she managed to be launched, it was a disappointment not to get the men. When the secretary called all the crew together to the Reading Room, he specially wanted to hear from Philloo's lips the reason they had not been the first boat off. Philloo then made the statement that the private boat was a lighter boat, the gangway was an easier place to get down than their own slipway, and also there was a large number of men willing to help launch her. The secretary wasn't too pleased with this excuse and said to him, 'Cooper, I hope you realise what this means. The report I will have to make to the Inspectors will certainly not be in your favour and I can assure you, you will get a severe reprimand from the Institution'. After this stern warning, he paid out all the money that was due to the men including Philloo. With that the old chap shuffled his feet and said 'Thank you sir. I'm sure I'm most grateful.' And he went down the steps to the crowd waiting below for him.

They all knew he had had to report to the Governors and wondered what the outcome was. Amongst this group of fishermen was old Tom 'Barnes' Cooper, coxswain of the *Augusta*. Chuckling to himself, he called Robert Cooper on one side. 'Well, how did you get on?' said Tom 'Barnes', expecting to hear the worst. 'Alright' replied Philloo, 'I didn't do at all badly, in fact I got on very well. I'm going to get a reprimand', quite pleased with himself. 'Reprimand?' said Tom, 'Do you know what that is?' 'Yes,' said Philloo 'it's one of those things what you hang up on the wall, isn't it?' 'You silly old fool,' replied Tom Barnes, 'it's a telling off and probably a lot worse!'

Now this yarn I heard from old 'Coley' Cooper one evening when a crowd had gathered outside the *Henry Ramey* shed and I wondered if it was all true. Old Grandfather was alive at that time, although getting old, but I brought up the subject of the 'reprimand' and he was quite happy to laugh about it. 'Ah,' he said 'they all had a good laugh and thought I was going to get the sack, but they knew better than that and kept me on till after I was well over sixty'.

Just before he died I went to see him one night. It was getting late and he had been poorly for a long time. His daughter, Sarah, my mother, would go in every day to see how he was and take him some broth or something if she could. That night when I called, he was feeling very cold, so I thought I would go and tell my mother how he was. She said 'I'll make him a good drop of hot whisky', which she did and I carried it around to him. His remark was 'Whatever have she sent me? This don't seem much, only a little drop of hot sugar water. Whatever was she a doing of?' That was the last time I saw my grandfather. A few days later he died. His funeral was at Upper Town; he was born at Easter and died at Easter in 1909. The day they took him to his last resting place the snow lay thick and heavy on the ground. When we went up the lane to Upper Sheringham churchyard, the hedges and trees were covered in snow and it was piled high in drifts.

My father's parents, Granny and Grandfather 'Joyful'
Joshua Henry and Sarah West

13. Father and Son

(Father's story continued)

After fishing out of Grimsby, we returned to Sheringham in the early part of 1920 and my partners and I decided to have a new boat built - a whelker of 3 tons called the *Little May*. Besides going for whelks, we went for dog fish and codling. There was plenty to be had in those days. We got our whelks for the same merchant as before, Mr H. R. Johnson, who used the old whelk coppers near the Driftway. These buildings were a row of sheds that faced westwards and the boiling coppers with tall chimneys pouring out the black smoke were ready for our return. Quite a few of the Shannocks worked there, 'Ben Tim' Smith, Russell Johnson, Joe Farrow and the Grice brothers and Ernie Grimes with many others. Sacks of whelks were collected by the railway horse and dray daily and went by rail to London, Clacton, Southend and other large towns. Sheringham at that time was one of the largest suppliers of whelks in the country. At one time a Sheringham football team took as its badge a golden whelk worn on their shirts. Also I think some crested china was made. The whelkers, about twenty large (22ft) motor boats, each had a crew of three. Amongst the main boats were *Liberty, Welcome Home, Admiral Beatty* and *White Heather*.

Then when Weybourne Camp started in 1936 it was a bit of a job to go out to sea when the artillery guns were in action. We got some compensation when the grounds were closed, so there wasn't much whelking done after this. But a few boats did try to carry on. I carried on for about nine years, then my only son was coming to the age for going to sea. He had been interested in it for some time and was always messing about in boats with his chums. My wife and I talked about it for a long time and wondered if it was the best thing for him to follow in my footsteps. Most of the sons of fishing families did this - there was little else to do - or went to work on the land. Once the decision had been made, we approached my father for the use of the *Olive*, which he owned and had been using with old 'Gayton' Cooper, and during those years it was pleasant to go with my son. He was very eager to learn and could soon haul and bait up the crab pots, but as I could remember how hard it was for me when I started with my father, I didn't let him do the hauling until he was a lot stronger. Then my brother Bob came to see us and we talked about him coming in to join us and share the work which seemed to me alright. About this time, my

The launching of the Acadia in 1927. L to R: Father, Bob, Uncle Bob and two cousins Jack and Henry aboard.

father had a fine boat built in Johnny Johnson's boat shed in 1928, named *Acadia* and this boat we used and went all three together. My father was a bit concerned because he told me I had probably made a mistake and might find my brother difficult to get along with, but I felt that things would be alright. So we drifted along and had our disagreements and minor upsets but things never got too bad. We cooked and boiled all the whelks ourselves, taking them to the station to go to the various markets.

Then came the Second World War and my son like a lot of others, got called up into the Royal Navy and had to report to Lowestoft. So I looked around for another partner. There was not a lot to be earned at sea and as I have already told you, most of us went to work clearing woods and working on aerodromes.

As the war ended and things were beginning to get back to normal, my son was demobbed. He went in one boat with my brother and it was decided that the two nephews Jack and Henry should start off their lives at sea with me and we all worked well together like this. I was very happy to have them with me; they were two green hands, but very happy and eager to learn, longing to be at sea.

I never regretted taking them; they were exceptionally good and soon learnt my ways, so this arrangement suited us all. My brother and son were catching the crabs and lobsters and we were going off for the whelks.

Now these two nephews of mine are married with families of their own and have been working together all their lives. The eldest one, Henry, known as 'Joyful' to everyone, is at the time of my writing this coxswain of the lifeboat and his brother Jack is bowman. They look like being the last of the 'Joyfuls' to follow the sea, as their sons have been to Universities studying for better prospects.

Young people realise that there is little future for the coming generations to earn a living at sea. In those day which I recall, it was a hard life with not a lot of reward, strenuous and very often labour in vain; bad weather and gales would tear our gear and lines to pieces, and we would often lose most of our gear at the start of the season. Nowadays, things are certainly a bit better as the new boats have good strong engines and haulers are installed which can pull up the pots, thus halving the toil. It is a far cry from the earlier days when they went with me learning the ropes.

One day, when we had been whelking and were on our way home, the weather hadn't been too fine, a bit foggy with a ground swell. As we made the land about abreast of Cley, coming easterly along the shore, we espied a small motor-boat ashore with the seas breaking right over her. We decided to go as near as we could but it was too dangerous to get close as the weather was deteriorating every minute and every moment's delay meant trouble for ourselves in getting safely ashore. So we called out to them to let go of an anchor as the tide was flowing up, and I knew if he was on what we called the Out Bank

Making crab-pots, Bob aged 16
and May aged 9.

with the swells coming in, he would be knocked further into deeper water. He didn't want us to leave him but we explained that we would alert the lifeboat. However, before the lifeboat could get there, he was off the Bank alright and quite safe. I think the name of the boat was the *Crown* or something like that.

The days I have recalled were shortly after the ending of the Second World War. My own son had returned from service in the Royal Navy. Most of his time had been on boom defence vessels at Plymouth and Liverpool during the blitz when the bombing of these ports was at its height - Liverpool all ablaze and Plymouth completely gutted - he said how terrible it was when they went ashore.

Now that I am telling you about the lifeboats, you never know what sort of treatment you are going to get from the crews aboard the vessels in question. You never know whether you're going to be sworn at or ridiculed, especially if the lifeboat gets called off to them and the crew believe they are not in any imminent danger. I know myself what they said to the lifeboat crew one Saturday night. It happened to be the *Henry Ramey* boat that was launched to a large steamer, about a mile north of Sheringham. The weather was nicely fine and that was the reason we did not take the Institution boat, the *J. C. Madge*.

Well, the lifeboat got alongside the vessel when the skipper shouted out he didn't want any help from the lifeboat crew and the best thing they could do the next day (which of course was the Sunday) was to go to Chapel and pray 'for those in Peril on the Sea'.

When the vicar heard about this, he took it upon himself to write to the owners, complaining of their rudeness and behaviour. Another time, both lifeboats were launched to a small tanker ashore at Beeston Hill. Once again, it was a fine day and this time too, they said they didn't want any assistance. Both of the lifeboats lay alongside, awaiting events. Suddenly the Captain came and had a look over the side and then he hailed both boats, saying 'I know what you two b----- are hoping for. I've been in the same game myself. I bet if I could see your old women now, they're holding out their aprons ready for the salvage money!' Then after a while he came aft again and shouted out 'Do any of you know "Darky" at Whitstable?' Of course we all knew who he was talking about as he had been an old local and had gone to Whitstable to live. The skipper said he lived next door to him and it was their home base, so a few minutes after this conversation, the coxswain called out to him suggesting running an anchor out, whereupon the mate said 'How much would you charge for that?' The coxswain replied 'One hundred pounds.' 'Good God,' said the mate, 'you'd better take the old b----- that's as much as she's worth.' At this point the crew had another look over the side and could see the water was getting deeper. The engineer was given orders to start her up astern and see if they could get her off. It looked very doubtful but after about 15 minutes or so, she gradually managed to refloat herself - the mate and crew having a great laugh at our expense, and as she steamed away, they gave us some jeering words - 'Never mind, better luck next time, mates'. But sadly to say, some 6 to 8 months later the same little tanker went down, during a very bad gale as she was approaching the Humber. Whether they were the same crew as we had launched for we never knew. Some years later 'Darky' came back to Sheringham and he remembered the captain and mate very well.

Well, I think I must mention Henry Blogg of Cromer. He became a famous coxswain, but was always a very quiet man. He never gave much away. He was the sort of chap that kept himself to himself. Of course there was always a great rivalry between the two towns Sheringham and Cromer, especially when it came to the local football teams. In their matches together, they almost always got to fighting, sometimes getting on to the pitches. Henry Blogg and some of the Cromer crew would attend these occasions, and many a swearing match would result, long before the game. I well remember one occasion, when the police arrived and made us 'Shannocks' go one way and the Cromer crabs the other. It was usually like this when the two towns met in the North Norfolk League or for the Queen's Cup. Strangely enough when there was any disaster or tragedy at sea, they would then be the best of friends and help each other as much as they could. Their boats or men would come to our assistance, and if there had been loss of life, all men would co-operate together to find gear or the bodies of fishermen lost from the boats.

There was some wonderful work done by the Cromer lifeboat. The rescue of the Dutch oil tanker *S.S. Georgia* which got aground on the dreaded Haisbro' sands on 22nd November, 1927. This vessel broke in two and the after part drifted North as far as Beeston Hill near Sheringham. The Cromer boat launched and went in search. When they reached the after part of the ship, they found no one on board. By this time, the weather had turned very rough and Coxswain Blogg decided to take his boat to Yarmouth as he was unable to get back on to the pier at Cromer and by this time, the Gorleston lifeboat had been launched to rescue the men on the other half of the tanker, now aground on the Haisbro'. The coxswain of the Gorleston boat could see the crew on board but as the sea was worsening all the time, he dare not go alongside until the weather abated. The lifeboat stood by the stricken vessel all night. In the morning, the weather had certainly calmed a bit, so then an attempt was made to rescue the men, some of whom were now in the rigging. Unfortunately, the rope became entangled in the propeller, thus making the rescue impossible. Passing at that time, was the Trinity house vessel and realising what had happened, Cromer lifeboat was called up and soon on its way. The weather was getting better every minute, which was lucky for Blogg; he was able to get all the crew of the *Georgia* safely on to his boat and back to Cromer. How quickly the weather can change. It was very disappointing for the Gorleston crew who had stood by all those hours, not to have been able to rescue the men. The church bells at Cromer were rung and hundreds of people lined the cliffs and promenade.

Well that is how it goes sometimes. There has always got to be a lot of luck in these things but what I am going to write about is another story. It happened one Boxing Day. The Cromer boat got a call so many miles North East from their station and let me say, when I heard the Cromer boat was off, I could hardly believe it, because I had never seen it so rough and blowing a fierce gale, and to crown it all, they were recalled, as they were not wanted after all. So Blogg was in a predicament. He knew he wouldn't get her on to the pier and would have to make his way to Yarmouth or try to get to the Humber. It was the latter he decided upon and they proceeded to make for the Humber. My old friend Jack Davies of the Cromer crew said he had never seen it so bad, the worst he had experienced. When they got to the mouth of the Humber, Blogg decided not to go in as the Bull light was showing a red light at the entrance. One of the other crew members, George Balls, who had worked here previously, felt it would be alright to go in and made this remark to Blogg. But the coxswain would not risk the lifeboat until daybreak. It was one of the longest trips Blogg had had to undertake in such appalling weather.

The last time I saw Henry Blogg was when I was with my son. We were off after our lobster pots, somewhere East of Runton, and had baited up and were setting our last pots towards home, when Bob said 'Turn the boat back again, I now saw someone jump out of a canoe'. So we started up the engine, quickly putting our last pots in. By that time, I could see the object in the water. I said 'I think that's a Cromer man hauling his gear'. 'Yes' replied my son 'but I did see someone either fall out of that canoe, or jump. We'd better just make certain.' So away we went, and lo and behold, clinging on to a buoy was this young girl. She was looking very frightened and glad to see us. I shouted to her 'Hang you on, we'll have you in a minute'. We then managed to get alongside of the buoy and had her swiftly aboard our boat. Needless to say, she was now looking a lot happier. We both asked her whatever had happened. She explained that she was being blown out to sea in the canoe, and she couldn't control it. She knew that her best bet was to try to get on to some object if possible and the buoy was the first thing she sighted. She could see her canoe - it was by this time quite a mile away and going fast - so we told the young lady we would try and get it for her and tow it back. Luckily, we were able to get a rope on to the canoe and then we headed back to Cromer. Of course, we didn't want to go ashore there so decided to look around and see if there was any Cromer boat which would take her ashore. She was only 17 years old and her family must have been getting alarmed by this time.

Luckily for us, we saw Blogg in his boat and we gave him a shout. He came alongside and we transferred the young girl into his boat with the canoe in tow. Then we headed for home. Strangely enough, we didn't hear any more about it for a long time; I think I was a bit surprised that her parents did not come into Sheringham to see us, not that we expected a reward, that was the last thing we would have accepted anyway, but felt that it must have been a dreadful worry for her parents when she didn't turn up on the beach. We were only too glad to have been on the spot when it happened. But all ended well. About a week or so later there was a letter sent to the local paper from Enfield, thanking us both for rescuing his daughter and that was the last time I saw Henry Blogg.

Most of those years, I went to sea with my son Bob until he decided to go with a younger chap. I joined a partnership, some of whom were like me and getting on in years. We all pulled together very well. Our summer days meant going after the crabs and lobsters and taking them to our various merchants, fetching the bait when it arrived at the station every day, and cutting up the bait for the next day's catch. In between these activities, we took visitors off in the boats. During the holiday season, hundreds of visitors were arriving in Sheringham and we undertook to take them off 'tripping'. They all enjoyed this. We used long wooden stools as ramps for the folks to walk on and get into the boats. Some old dears, we carried on our backs. It was real hard work, especially if we had been up early in the morning to our pots, but it was another way of making some money. The boats were often overloaded and gradually there was some concern at how many should be accommodated on each trip. So the authorities told us we could only take so many.

Eventually, it died out. We also took off fishing parties for the afternoon, for dabs or bass. Often we got the same people coming to us year after year.

It was in later years when I was in poor health, that my son went with his partner Jimmy Bishop, nicknamed 'Chibbles'; they were also known as 'the inseparables' and acquired another name which every one knew them by. This was 'Cake and Custard' and originated from one having had patches put on his trousers that looked like pancakes! There was always someone with a quick wit who could supply these nicknames.

Then I had to go into the Norfolk and Norwich Hospital undergoing three serious operations. I thought I would never go back to sea again and was very ill for two or three years. The surgeons at the Hospital were very good to me and assured me that they had prolonged my life for another ten years if I was sensible and took life a bit easy. I was then 65 years old. I could never thank the nurses and doctors enough for all they did for me. Gradually I got stronger and longed to be at sea again, but the doctors were still concerned and I had to visit the Norwich Hospital for a long time.

Luckily Mr H. E. West, 'Downtide' as we knew the family, owned a fish shop in the High Street and he suggested that I went and helped boil the crabs. This suited me alright - it was a great help to earn a bit of money again, but most of all to be amongst the men who were going to sea, to hear all the yarns and jokes. Mr West employed me in a light capacity, scrubbing and boiling the crabs and lobsters for his shop. I enjoyed myself! The following year, now feeling more myself, I began to think longingly of getting back to sea, but also felt that I might be a hindrance to my son or anyone who was younger than myself. As time went by, a young Sheringham chap needed someone to go to sea with him and he came to see me and being eager to go, I agreed. He only went to sea when it suited him - as many times he was off on his jaunts to the City. Now began a period of my life which was the most frustrating, the most annoying and yet the most comical time I ever knew at sea. So this is how I became partner to P---. I overlooked his many faults; he was one of the most peculiar partners to have, I felt like swearing at him and cursing, but actually we never did have any quarrels but there were times when I swore I would never go to sea with him again!

How well I remember going to sea with P---. I could write a book about him. He was hopeless at sea and he wouldn't get up in the morning. The other fishermen would be down on the beach getting their boats off and they would be fed up with him. They would say 'If it wasn't for you Joyful, we wouldn't help him at all' so I would go to his house at least a half an hour before we had to get our boat down, just to spur him on.

Sometimes I would stand in the road under his little bedroom window and shout to him, did he know what the time was? The next door neighbours would open their windows and complain about being woken up so b--- early every morning, saying it was a damned nuisance, he wouldn't get himself out of bed, but no matter what I did, he wouldn't stir himself; it never bothered him how much commotion was going on.

Then I might shout out that I was going home, I was fed up with waiting about for him, I wasn't going to put up with it any longer. All the while this one sided conversation was going on, the fishermen were rolling about with laughter. They could see the funny side of it which was more than I could. By this time I was losing my patience, also my temper, and would end up by rushing into his little kitchen where he would be sitting with a pot of tea in front of him. I would grab his long hair and try to pull him out. Of course, this suited all those outside who were hoping for such an event. His long-suffering wife would remark how sorry she was, but there was little she could do.

Then we would go to sea and he didn't know the first thing about crabs, or the right sort to bring ashore. Finally, the Fishery Officer took me on one side and said 'Henry Willie, you must not let him have anything to do with the crabs as he does not know what he's doing' so with this I decided to let him do the hauling and I managed to look after the crabs. But this wasn't too successful. He would be alright if the sea was moderately calm, but if there was a tide running and it was particularly hard, or he had to use the engine, he was hopeless. I would tell him hundreds of times and shew him what to do but he would still prove useless.

He could never remember where his pots were. I had always kept my shanks of pots separate from his and apart from mine. We had come a bit further to the north to haul his. I sat in the boat having hauled mine and baiting up the pots again so was letting him carry on. After a while, we came to his marker buoys. They were marked with two very large initials of his name, but he went sailing past them to my amazement. I never said anything, just watched and waited. All of a sudden, he said to me 'I thought we should have seen my buoys by now, didn't you?' I just looked at him and said 'You nearly hit the b---s, if they had been b--- mines, we should have been blown to hell by now.' He just looked at me, stunned like and then slowly said 'How ever did I miss them?' I said 'You're half asleep three parts of your time and don't know north from south'.

Well, I called him several names in those few years I went with him, but he never answered me back. He really was the last straw. He was more interested in going off on his jaunts to the City and London, where he said he had got a lot of big business to attend to.

And so my days at sea were drawing to a close. I had had pleasant and happy times, very worrying times and times of despair, but still the sea called me and had been my whole life. I had seen a great change, both in boats, partners, various aspects of fishing, changes of gear, rowing and sailing, later to engines to ease the toil. The sea is a hard task master. It bends us to its will, breaks and takes, ever the stronger ceaseless and surging, but always one feels close to God upon the waters. I was still earning my living at the age of 76 and finding it harder to carry on. My wife was now in poor health and I had to leave the sea to those more able to carry on. I had to be content to listen to their tales.

Holiday-makers
ready for a trip, 1931

14. Mother's Recollections

Father has been recalling his everyday life at sea in these few chapters, but when I was with them both in their little cottage, my mother would often help to correct a date, or person, place, or circumstance. She had a wonderful memory and a remarkable wit with a very dry sense of humour. She was always ready to see the funny side of life and most especially made anyone welcome who called at their house, whether it was some one they knew or a perfect stranger.

In her younger days she was a small figure of five foot, with dark auburn-coloured hair, a round face and a twinkle in her eye - very smartly dressed when she went off to chapel each Sunday.

Born into an old fishing family by the name of Cox, her very early years were spent in tiny cottages called Cox's Yard, now since disappeared into modern development, situated behind West's fish shop in High Street, Sheringham. This tiny yard and its cottages were all used by the same families. Later, her parents, Robert and Hannah Cox moved to another small triangular yard, consisting of five or six cobblestoned cottages of two up and two down. Here lived more fishing families and in the corner of this yard was a whelk copper where her father boiled the whelks. A large gate led out into Station Road. We know this area now as the site of today's 'Little Theatre'.

She had an elder sister Eliza and a young brother. They all went to a tiny little dame school opposite the cottages. It was run by a Mrs Wilson and was the only school where they had any learning. Two steps led down to a small room where these few scholars went, only about ten or twelve pupils. Their coats would all be thrown on to a couch or chair, and according to my mother, they learnt very little.

Robert John Cox ('Sugar') and his family. L to R: John, Eliza & Mary Ann.

She admitted when she left school she could not read or write! But, being of an eager and enquiring mind, she soon rectified this, as in her later years she was an avid reader, interested especially in politics; she went to all political meetings and could turn her hand to anything in her home.

Very often, when they were all in school, her father would come over the road and knock on the window and tell them all that there was a circus in town or a dancing bear. As a result of his interference and quite disregarding the governess they were all let out. So much for education! Her father paid 6d per week for her to go to this school. Her small school book is still in my possession. Other pupils at the same time were Maud and Arabella Swallow, whose father was the landlord of the Railway Tavern now the Robin Hood and John and Henry West who later became farmers near Aylmerton.

She started school at the age of three and left when she was about ten or eleven years old as her father thought she would be more use on his land helping with the weeding. He hired land from Mr Upcher on the Upper Town Road which later on was to become the Recreation Ground and employed several men to help with the corn, also growing mangels and swedes. In one corner of the field was a large barn. A threshing machine would be hired to thresh the corn and stacks would be built. Mother had to hold the horses and take them where they were needed. Often she and her sister Eliza and her cousins had to crawl about on hands and knees weeding the rows of carrots and turnips, doing the whole length of the field in the heat of the sun; sometimes they were careless and didn't do them thoroughly, then one of the old men would come along and say, 'You aren't doing them properly, you're being a sluverer, you'll het ta du them agin', whereupon they did!

Their next move was to a house in Church Street. A double-fronted house, called Fern Lea. This was, according to mother, a very large house and a nice one. Today this is Lloyds Bank. After the family had lived here for a short time, they moved into Elm Croft in Waterbank Road where most of the houses on the same side were lived in by members of the Cox family. I have heard her say it was a private road and once a year a chain was put across at the south end. In those days, there was a stream running the whole length of the road and banks of primroses. At the lower end of this road were stables where they kept some horses and a landau which the family used.

Her father, nicknamed 'Sugar', was in business with his brother-in-law, dealing in fish, whelks and coal and was constantly going backwards and forwards to Norwich, or

Cromer, in search of business. Sometimes he took mother and Eliza and their cousin with him. The two latter would always wear the very latest fashion and enjoyed trips into the city with him, but when there he would go off on his jaunts around the various inns and hostels to do 'business' as he said. Mother often voiced her disapproval, so next time she was left behind.

Sheringham families in the early days were inter-related, and in such a small community, so tightly knit, it was impossible to find any that were not connected to each other either by marriage or as cousins; young husbands were drowned and widows re-married and brought up step-children. Some married two or three times, especially the fishermen who lost young wives in childbirth. The Cox family date back to 1600 and probably before that. Doing research several years after my parents died I discovered that Hannah and Robert Cox, my grandparents, were cousins, descended from the Robert Cox born in 1754. Practically all were to become fishermen.

Whenever I had the time, I would listen to their tales of Sheringham and its characters. They would describe what the town was like. High Street was mostly small cottages with little gardens and railings outside. The farm yard for the Upchers had a large gate leading out of it and old 'Rushie Loades', team man for the Hall, would bring the cattle across to the reservoir - this is now the Woolworths building. Opposite the house called Fern Lea Mother said there was a large meadow and horses would be turned out there at night. To the west of this were some allotments, cornfields and haystacks.

Mother would make us laugh when she would tell of going down Wyndham Street as a small child with her mother to use the old-fashioned box mangle which was housed by Mrs Paul Reynolds. In the first house next to theBakery (Leeder's) was old Mr Honeyman, then Paul Reynolds, and here was to be found one of the old box mangles. There were three in the village and they were charged one penny to use them. The women folk would gather here with their offspring and exchange all the local gossip. One such mangle is in the Strangers Hall Museum in Norwich. The mangle consisted of a large box worked with a large handle fastened to a roller which propelled the box of stones back and forth. Huge stones were obtained from the beach to fill it and all manner of linen could be laid in it. The box itself was large enough for the young children to ride on it whilst the women gossiped, all the children taking turns. It was looked upon as a day out!

Little boys wore frocks and pinafores until they were nearly five years old and women wore shawls over their heads and blue and white aprons in the morning and what is known as print aprons in the afternoon.

We can hardly realize the difference in the beaches, how much they have changed. My parents would describe the fairs and swing boats down on the sands in front of the present sea wall, and they would tell of stalls filled with all manner of goods: grapes, fruit, sweets and some toys especially at Easter time. There were rock stalls and games. Now we see the sea breaking on to the promenade at that corner by the Crown Inn at almost every tide.

An open air Dutch auction was held very regularly on Lifeboat Plain by some folks whose name was Pope. They owned a large horse-drawn cart and hawked various items around the town. Paraffin lamps were suspended on the cart as it made its way around the little side streets to light the way and it would end up on the Square near the Crown Pub, where everything would be laid out on the ground for display before the auction started. Their wares consisted of plates, tea services and dinner services, china and glass and all sorts of bric à brac. They had a daughter who died in a caravan fire.

Many old characters lived in the little cottages, some quite eccentric. One in particular was 'Tailor Love' or 'Luff'. He was evidently a tailor, and he kept a small shop right opposite the Two Lifeboats Hotel (then the Temperance Hotel) near the cliff edge. It had a small fence or railing around his tiny yard. He was a very queer old chap and would chase anyone away who dared to peer into his window. He was looked on as the Town Crier, going around the few streets calling out the news or announcements. He was also the Town Barber and when anyone went to have a hair cut, he was put into an old armchair and an apron placed round his neck, but when the customer lay back and looked up to the ceiling, all he could see above him was rows of rabbit skins, now drying and suspended from nails and hooks. Hundreds were hanging from the rafters. Needless to say, there were plenty of flies! When anyone needed the doctor, it meant a long run to Cromer to fetch him; 'Taylor Love' was quite willing to do this in all weathers and for this errand he received the princely sum of a whole shilling.

Living next door was old Mary Greet. She was the first person to sell Sunday newspapers from her little front room and this became a well-known establishment for Sunday papers run by the 'Lark' Bishop family. Besides selling papers, she took on the job of pulling people's teeth. She was as good as any dentist, and most of the village folks went to her for their various ailments and some cures were effected. My grandmother Cox had her teeth pulled by her at a very early age. Mary Greet's family seem to have originated from Cornwall; her father was a coastguard here in the early years.

Another character was 'Old Charlie Frog'. He was around when some of us were in our childhood. His proper name eludes me but his job was to come around the street at night with what was called the 'muck cart'. It was lit with lanterns on the side and about eleven o'clock at night he emptied the dry toilets.

Quite near to Slippers Loke near West Cliff, was a small sweet shop and all manner of goods owned by a Mr Smith. The locals had given him the strange nickname of 'Old Smooth Eye'. Father once went inside with a few of his cousins when very young and took a big box of chocolates. The old fellow managed to see him doing this out of the corner of his eye and grabbing hold of him, marched him home under protest, whereupon he was soundly beaten by his own father and told never to go out with those ---- boys again.

Both parents loved to recall the days of the Harvest Frolics and Camp Meeting days on Beeston Common. The latter festivities would commence in the town centre; a large crowd would gather at the Town Clock - all manner of folks and of various religions, from wide and far with musical instruments, singing hymns and praying. They would proceed along the High Street then Wyndham Street into Paper Mill Lane, on their way to the Top Common where old Mr Reynolds of the Priory Farm would have ready a couple of wagons for the various preachers to use as a pulpit. There would be several preachers from nearby districts and hundreds of people would congregate around the farm carts to listen to these people, preaching and singing. Both Mother and Father would remark how wonderful it was to listen to these old preachers who needed no notes but could speak from their hearts. Some of the company would now and again give their testimonials. People would sit about on the grass and enjoy the hymn singing. After all this was over, the whole procession would make its way back to the chapel in Station Road where they all partook of bread and water, some of them so earnest that they would swoon and fall about.

But the Grand occasion of the year was at the end of Harvest, when all was safely gathered in. This was the Harvest Frolics for which Reynolds' barn on the Cromer Road was used. This barn has now sadly fallen into ruins - all that is left is the cobbled stone wall. Another barn used was the one belonging to old Mr Spenton at Beeston Hall Corner. For weeks the women had been preparing the pies, home made bread, ham, cheeses and beef. There was plenty of beer and ale. Tumbrils were used to bring all the food along to the barns and people came from miles around. Sometimes these frolics lasted for three or four days - some of the men were drunk for days!

Mother's grandparents on her mother's side of the family, John and Elizabeth Cox, lived in the third little cottage down Lobster Lane as it was then called, later to become Gun Street. They had a sad life; they had six children and two sons who became fishermen were drowned at sea. Robert Henry in 1909 was lost off Bacton and left a wife and two babies. Much earlier, in 1879, their young son John, aged 18, was drowned when eight Sheringham men failed to return after going out fishing, all in one large vessel. In the following days most of the bodies came ashore. John each day searched the shore for his son, and then early one morning at daybreak he found him amongst the nets.

My mother loved visiting her grandparents and hearing their tales. She said she would sit by the fire and often had to get the bellows out of the coal cupboard. The old lady would say 'Put them on your lap and work them up and down against the bars of the grate, you will soon have a good fire'. Mother would say they were all she could lift, but she did it. She would often be sent to buy some lamp oil at the little shop on Lifeboat Plain, so the tiny lamp could be filled and the wick trimmed. Often it would smoke the glass and you couldn't see across the room. They did all their sewing and knitting by the aid of rush lights or lamps, yet they did the most beautiful needlework, embroidering the mens' shirts and doing fine tucks on their nightdresses and blouses. All the ladies knitted fishermen's 'ganseys' as did the young girls. They would use the knitting sheaths (wooden and hand carved) tucked into the sides of their aprons and could knit so fast, often finishing a 'gansey' in two or three weeks, all with their special patterns.

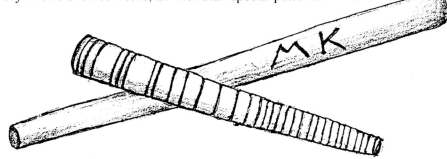

Knitting sheaths

One day when the fire wouldn't draw the grandmother told Mary Ann to go and buy two pennyworth of gunpowder at the little shop. She said 'Go and see old Sophie and we'll get the fire to go before long'. Mother went to get it and Grandmother threw a few grains on the smouldering coals. There was a huge bang and sparks and coal dust flew every where. The bottom of the grate flew out and when they looked in the mirror, all the front of their hair had been singed, and eyebrows too!

All around in the little cottages on Lifeboat Plain were various members of the same families. Mother would say how their places were always kept very clean. The floors were either tiled or made with bricks and hardly any matting on the floors. They would get sand from the beach in pails and sprinkle this on the tiles, then each day it would be swept up.

When the Salvation Army first started it was in the Boat House on Lifeboat Plain. This was the place where the Emery family built several large boats and the large room above called the Net Loft was taken over by the newly arrived Salvationists. Most of the families, children and adults, attended these meetings having to go up a ladder from the outside of the building to reach the first floor. There were very large congregations but not everyone wanted the new religion, especially the publicans - it looked like interfering with their trade. So whenever the 'Army' band played and sang at their open air meetings, some publicans would get out their horses and carts and drive right through the 'Army' ring with many fights and arguments.

Then there was grand sports held at sea. Boat races, sand sports and also the *Augusta* and later the *Henry Ramey* boats were used to take part in some of the activities like the 'greasy pole'. This was often the last event of the day but eagerly awaiting as participants would try their skills. A very large straight tree or oar would be lashed to the lifeboat across the middle of the boat and very well greased with thick yellow grease and on the end of this was a small box with a trapdoor containing a pig. If the participants could overcome the grease and fat and get to the end of the pole, touching the stick which allowed the release of the trapdoor, the poor pig would splash into the sea and be won! There were always the same contestants for this and very often won by the same man every year. After many years, they did away with using a live pig though the prize was the same, but for many years a poor animal had to endure this torment.

Another annual event was the Tug of War between the fishermen and landsmen. On Shrove Tuesday every year, the children who went to the Beeston Road School went with their teachers to Beeston Hill. It had two hills then, but one has since gone into the sea. They would all be given oranges and from the top of the hill they would roll them down to race them to the bottom. This seems an echo from the ancient past and no one knows why it was done; maybe some ancient ritual.

The annual school treat was held in the park at Upper Sheringham, usually during June. All the children would get a bun and drinks of tea or lemonade. Races would be run and sweets would be given out. The ladies from the Hall and teachers from the Upper Sheringham School would organise this.

Life in Sheringham was simple indeed and their pleasures few. Often the loss of men and young boys at sea were to sadden their days, like the loss of Edward and Ernest West, one about 18, the other 20, sons of Augusta West, who lived in a little tiny cottage near the Two Lifeboats pub. They had been out fishing all day and to earn a bit more money, had gone again that night with their nets, but on coming home very tired, they were thought maybe to have fallen asleep in their boat, overturned and were drowned. When found, they were tangled up with their nets. Their young bodies were brought home and laid on the floor of the little front room.

Mother's life too, had its ups and downs. When she was a very young girl, her mother was ill for a very long time and she had to help nurse her and care for the home. Then her mother died of cancer and the family were sent to other near relatives to be brought up. John her brother, the youngest of the three children went to live with his Aunt Eliza, his father's sister. The eldest daughter Eliza went to live with her Grandmother Cox in Waterbank Road and Mother was sent to live with her Aunt Martha (Swatman) at Lowestoft, so the home was broken up and eventually Mother had to go into service in Bromley in Kent, working for a Capt. and Mrs Smith. She earned only a few shillings a month and only half a day off in two weeks. She hated it as she was badly treated by the Irish Cook and being miles away from home with no one she knew, she fretted but had to endure it. By then, her father had remarried to an Irish girl called Maria and it was decided that she and her brother John should go back home to live with him and his new wife. They had moved to Cromer by this time and at first things went along alright. But they didn't feel happy and threatened to run away. This came to a head one night when Maria threw the lamp at her husband and set the house on fire. In their fright, they ran all the way from Cromer to Sheringham in the middle of the night during a terrible thunder-storm, to their grandparents' home where they were taken in and stayed the rest of their time.

She eventually went to work for a Mr and Mrs Coombes who were headmaster and mistress of a boarding school for boys, situated at the top of Vincent Road. She found life here very pleasant and it was from here that she was married. This school was still there until the Second World War but under different teachers and headmasters.

Two pupils who attended the same small dame school as my mother,
Maud and Arabella Swallow. Their father was landlord
of the Railway Tavern

15. Nicknames and Characters

During their latter years, my parents collected together several nicknames well known to the 'Shannocks' and wrote them on scraps of paper or cardboard, as they recalled them. An intriguing part of Sheringham life was the habit of giving everyone a nickname - one of the main purposes was to identify the families, there being several families with the same surname and even with the same Christian name. So at least, if they had a nickname they could be easily identified and in those days one knew them more by their nicknames than their proper names. In fact, so well known were their nicknames all along the coast and far inland, often one didn't know who was being spoken of if proper names were used. At one time, there were about twenty families all surnamed West living in Beeston Road!

Newcomers to Sheringham are very interested in these names and often ask how they are acquired. The origins of the names are difficult to ascertain. When asked, some of the fishermen or holders of these names do not know why they were so called. Many of them had two nicknames such as 'Philloo' Cooper who was also known as 'Anyhow'. Quite a number were prefixed by the word 'Old' or 'Young' so there would be 'Old Black Bob' and 'Young Black Bob' or 'Old Shot Tail' and 'Young Shot Tail'.

The names were handed down from generation to generation; thus would the families be known and identified 'Old Downtide' West,'Young Downtide' and Molly 'Downtide'. Maybe some characteristic or expression of speech, an action of work, or acquisition of a habit, would start the handle to his or her name. If you ask the family of the 'Downtide' Wests how they got their name, they will tell you it was because one of the older generation, when he went off fishing one morning, made the remark that he was 'rowing up-tide'.

'Shot tail' another West, was always busy at his gear with his shirt hanging out of his trousers, and some wise one referred to a crab shooting its shell when he got his nickname.

I have already said how the 'Joyful' Wests got their nickname, so suffice it to say that the first Joshua Henry, who sung the same hymn repeatedly with 'Joyful' words in the first line, soon acquired his handle. They also say he was a bit of a mournful character!

One of the Cox family had the peculiar name of 'Bread alone' and he would often get up in chapel and give a sermon, and invariably he would take the same text from the Bible 'Man shall not live by bread alone', so of course, it didn't take the others long to give him that title. But strangely other members of the same family were not known by that name, as his brothers were known as 'Leather' and 'Latter day' and 'Cut the Wind'.

The first lifeboat called the *Duncan*, the R.N.L.I. boat helped to give the nickname 'Duncan' to the Cooper family. Although 'Philloo' and other Coopers had been in the crew of this boat, it was to the son of Robert 'Philloo' Cooper that the name 'Duncan' was given.

Once when I enquired of Jimmy 'Paris' West (another well known character) how he got his name, he replied that he didn't know - it had just been handed down to him, but he did offer this explanation. He had been told that during the war between Prussia and France one of his ancestors as a little child was playing on some waste ground and running around and around, with a piece of wood cut like a rifle. When asked what he was doing, the boy said 'I am defending Paris'.

There certainly were many odd names, but all were used with pride and no malice, however rude or strange. Here are a few samples:-

The seats on the promenade would be filled with fishermen after their day's work was done. L to R: John 'Teapot' West, Henry Middleton, Father, Joe 'Drips' Little.

WESTS: Never sweat, Nails, Muggles, Squeezer, Gees-eye Squinter, Fiddy Tea Pot, Bumshee, Raleigh Darrick, Darky, Old Wench, Joyful, Hamshee, Braidy, Poverty, Patchy, Cutty, Old Harry Billy and others.
The West family was one of the largest in Sheringham and most of them were fishermen.

CRASKES: Billy 'Cutty', Lux; Old Buck, Hanna Gals, Tom Tads, Corgi, Old Bounce, Pork Pie, Coaches, Bells, Cock Robin, Billy Brick, Jizzy Dutch, Guineas, Munchy and others.

GRICES: King Kong, Old Cabbage, Old Cheese, Gotts, Mans, Baker, Chicken, Butter Ball, Corporal, Old Sarah Manns, Nanny Mink, Lolly, To Ro Bumshy, Young Chicken.

COX: Lettuce, Sugar, Patten, Duley, Cockney, Giffa, Daylights, Strong Arms, Jehole.

COOPERS: Fannymere, Tippo, Pat a Key, Wooly, Nat, Jack Earl, Bob Hot, Tom Barnes, Coley, Anyhow, Old Ham, Gayton, Demon, Boy Tom, Key, Ham, Cock a Doodle Do, Fiddler, Mans Jordan, Sea Toad.

FARROWS: Lobster, Cow-weed, Salter, Two fee, Happy Bob, Bunny, Ridley, Spit-fire, Lassie, Wella Wella, Points, Hamrine, Lyga, Sally Binks, Kruger, Sacky, Joe Bottle, Cundle, To Jo, Old Cobbler, Hardweather.

FIELDS: Jimpson, Pearkue, Night hawk, Beef.

MIDDLETONS: Bennet, Tiddley, Munchy, Dingy, Old Mullet, Old Mink, Little Mullet, Old Pillock, Will-Eye, Morey Garty, Stallion Pig, Sandling.

PEGGS: Go-father, Kiff, Krongee, Gully, Fatty, Joe Arch, Pick, Hackie, Whistling Coon, Gay Jo, Gaffa, Nimshee, Denno, Marlbro, Scratchums, Mary Tearny, Nimshie, Heads.

LITTLES: Old Joe Drips, Stilly, Milka, Pongs, Old Will, Pinny, Twall, Pickles, Tails, Duffle Dick, Dowsey, Old Milka.

JOHNSON: Mace, Dippers, Uncle Dick, Spider, Billy Butcher, Money Ben, Knickers, Belcher, Old West, Boots, Bounce, Old Boots, Old Maggot, Kiffer, Rocky Ben, Pugalow, Gusta Buck, Honey Ben, Pringle, Pip, Pingy, Whelk Hagnett, and Cratchett, Snouts, Brandy and Bruff.

HANNAHS: Busseys, Dee Dee, Dunnahar, Jute, Slyly, and Haystack, Stoner.

LONGS: Slinks, Lingey, Pa Wagg, Old Bussey.

KNOWLES: Ikey, Blitchams, Jinny, Loose Gas, Sixer, Tucker, Peachey, Grandfather.

GRAYS: Jumbo, No bones, Ridley, Barwick.

EMERYS: Caller, Plug, Baltimore, Buffalo.

GRIMES: Honey, Saffron, and Jockey.
Other families were:-
'Sparrow' and 'Old Potter' Hardingham, 'Brigham's', 'Tar Wash', 'Lotion Tar'and 'Jack Tar' of the Bishop family and two members of the Reynolds family were always known as John 'Rook' and 'Grey Horse'.

Some of the strangest names were 'Greasy Hat' Scotter, 'Black Tad', 'Foggy Due', 'Charlie Frog', 'Tin Britches', 'Crackpot', 'Beechams Pills' (given to Chapman the chemist) 'Bite yer neck', 'Galloping Major', 'The Rude 'un', 'Old Rubber Gills' and 'Tater Billy'.

'Coaley' Cooper, coxswain of the *Henry Ramey* Upcher lifeboat obtained his name of 'Coaley' (later to be handed down to each member of his family) when he was a child; whilst playing amongst the boats, he thought he would be of help when he picked up a tar brush and proceeded to help tar the boats but he put far more tar upon himself than he did the boats. When the rest of the fishermen spotted him all covered with tar, they said 'Look, he's all Coaley Tar' so this name stuck to him, later to be shortened to 'Coaley'.

Another well known name in Sheringham is the 'Teapot' West family and there are two versions of how this nickname originated. On asking Lenny West of Beach Road, I was given this version. His grandfather, John Stephen West, was out in the Great Boats of those days and he rescued one of the earliest airmen who had come down in the sea. This was in the early days of aviation before the Royal Air Force. This airman was so grateful for being picked up, that he presented John West with a silver teapot and this then is the origin of the 'Teapot' West family. Other explanations of the same name all involve a teapot, silver or otherwise. Some say that one of the earlier Wests was given a silver teapot in recognition of a marriage which was not performed in the true faith.

Another fishing family had the nickname 'Chicken'. They were of the Grice family and all had various nick names as stated, but the origin of theirs is as follows.

Charlie 'Chicken' Grice was a well known fisherman of Sheringham who enjoyed playing jokes on people. A grand teller of tales and a bit of a singer too, he was very fond of a song called 'Delaney's chickens' and whenever the occasion arose, he would burst forth into song, especially if present at any local concert. Often he would be found on the stage, performing this 'chicken' song.

We can visualise the kind of characters that abounded in Sheringham of those days - a close-knit community, sadly altered in today's busy life. The habit of attaching nicknames to various members of the population is fast dying out, but still among the very few Shannocks, it is possible suddenly to be given one, especially if that person has done something or made a strange remark, or possibly been in the headlines. Woe betide him if it is not to his liking!

It is interesting to look at the customs of these folk who lived such simple lives. They fell into two categories. Most were devoutly religious and followed the Bible and its teachings to the letter. They read the Good Book often daily and followed its teaching - never doing anything at all on a Sunday. It was readily accepted by the young ones of the family that they should attend chapel two or three times during that day.

The other group of the Parish, and these were few, were very uncouth, surly individuals who used the local pubs and caused trouble in the village. There were often fights and drunken brawls.

My great great grandfather, Richard Cox, who was born in 1803 and lived in a tiny cottage north east of Beach Road with his wife Mary brought up seven sons and two daughters. All of these sons became fishermen, one of whom went to Wells to earn his living and his descendants too became fishermen and lifeboatmen of Wells. Richard, in his old age, went out preaching and reading the Bible to various people in their cottages. He was one of the few people who could read and write and was paid four shillings a week for this. He was accompanied by his son David, wherever they went preaching and singing.

On the other hand, my grandfather Robert (Sugar) Cox was much more inclined to enjoy the company of his fellow men in the local pubs, where he would play the violin, singing and spending as many hours as he could without a thought for the morrow.

Amongst the old characters that we all remember most is 'Go-father' Pegg, wearing his red chummy hat. He was the most enterprising individual and made the first beach hut for Sheringham beach. He benefited from this and was soon on the way to making a few more. He would fill up jars or bottles of sea water and sell it to the new holiday makers, professing that it would cure all sorts of aches and pains when applied to the limbs. If the tide was out when any of them were making enquiries, he would insist that it had done so much good that he was having a job to fill the bottles as the sea was getting less!

Another member of the Pegg family was Mary 'Tearney'. She was a spinster and at the time I remember lived in a tiny cottage in Chasteneys Yard. Mary had to augment her meagre income by doing work here and there for folks who employed her mostly to help with the washing or ironing. My mother had Mary to come and help with the washing on a Monday, mainly because it would help her (Mary) financially, as she felt sorry for her, and also because there was a lot of heavy washing to do in a fishing family. Mary would arrive about ten o'clock, her arms akimbo, wearing a black blouse, long sack apron and a shawl around her shoulders. Sometimes she had been attempting to cut her own hair and it wasn't always effective. Sometimes the hair would be standing out like a brush from the forehead. My brother and I, when we sat down to dinner (Mary always stayed all day and had dinner with us and sometimes tea) would look at each other and start giggling. My Mother would have none of this, telling us to be quiet and have our meal. Mary would enjoy her meal and hint every now and again at taking some home with her. Mother would say 'when you go home Mary, I will put some in a basin for you'.

When the washing and hanging-out ceased for a little while, Mother would put the kettle on to make a cup of tea. Mary was quite intrigued at this and always made the remark 'You make a lovely *Water would be everywhere.* cup of tea woman'. Mother would say 'Well, so can you Mary, can't you?' Mary's reply was that hers was never as hot as Mother's and how did she do it. 'Boil the kettle, Mary' said Mother. 'Oh' says Mary, 'I set alight to my paper in the grate and when that's burnt out I make the tea'. No doubt Mary had no idea if the kettle boiled.

She was always given the gear and clothes my father wore and would scrub away at these in the large tin bath on a small table in the scullery. The trouble was that she got so carried away with all this scrubbing, with the soap and lather that sometimes it would fly everywhere. Mother would say 'I'll have to put Mary outside in the yard next week, - the floor's all afloat with water and suds'. So on a fine day, her table was put outside.

She was always partial to my Mother's 'funters', a Norfolk name for buns or cakes and if we stopped to have a cup of tea, Mum would put some on a plate, whereupon Mary would say 'Gal' (meaning me) 'are you going to eat any of those?' Mother very cleverly would say 'I'll pack you a few up to take home for your supper when you go.' Poor Mary, she died, I believe, in the workhouse. I can remember very well going there to see her and she held my hand tightly.

Another female much tormented by us girls, lived in Tantivy Loke and was known as 'Pat-a-Key'. When we went past her door we never knew what was going to be thrown out of either the window overhead or the door. Alongside her little cottage was Angelina. Again one had to be very wary, because suddenly the back door would open and a panful of ash or warm coals would be hurled out at us. She was a very queer soul and would march up the street with her shawl wrapped tightly around her, speaking to no one, and it wasn't wise to speak to her either. It was rather sad when her husband died. It was said that she hadn't realized he was dead and he had lain on the sofa for three days, whilst she, 'Angelina', was doing her best to keep him warm, piling on the blankets in a small room with a roaring fire in the hearth.

Another Sheringham woman called Charlotte was also eccentric. She had been jilted or lost her lover early in life, but forever afterwards, she imagined that he was still around and would go into various shops and ask about him. Of course, this suited some of the assistants who would enlarge upon it to their own enjoyment. Poor Charlotte, she would be dressed all in black with beads and earrings, often carrying a large umbrella which she would wield about most menacingly. Some days she would be fairly rational, but when provoked or searching for her lover, she could get quite emotional. She was for ever asking us had we seen or heard about her fiancé 'Lord ---'. Many times we sent her scurrying off into the town, with our vague hints of just having sighted him.

The old fishermen, whom we knew as they went constantly about the various jobs at their nets or gear on the seashore, wore snowy white beards and many, with white hair and peaceful faces, reminded us of the old prophets. All had Bible names, such as Abraham, Obadiah, Daniel, Nathaniel, or Joshua. They would preach in chapel or church and needed little information from notes. They would expound from their own vivid experiences at sea, to bring the message home. One such was 'Old Downtide' West. When he preached, he would include bringing in the night's catch as if he had been himself on the shores of Galilee. In the Army band he marched, banging the big drum and waving his drum sticks on high as he beat to the music of the old hymns. It was a delight to see him. The chapels would then be filled to over-flowing when the 'Harvest of the Sea' service was held with row upon row of seated fishermen, all wearing their blue ganseys. The old men would call out the hymns and bang on the rostrum with their fists in fervour, to stir the congregation on, but they needed no such action as all joined in. It was the same at the Salvation Army Citadel, where for fifty years, a Harvest of the Sea had been held. Started by Henry Downtide West, this was the great occasion of the year. The Hall bedecked with nets and names of all the boats along the coast, with coxswains of lifeboat stations taking the service and grand old hymns sung.

Posing for the visitors. L to R: Uncle Bob 'Joyful', Father and Bob 'Rally' West.

16. Days of our Youth

In the thirties it was hard to find a job. Many who left school at the age of fourteen either went into service or to work behind the counter of one of the town's shops. Young girls of my age were lucky to get an apprenticeship to one of the large shops such as Rusts's. Their wage started at 2/6 per week, increasing to 7/6 after three or four years apprenticeship learning the trade; a very few finally became manageress or buyer.

I left school in 1931, first of all helping in the home waiting on table for visitors. I quite liked this as some of the day I could please myself. Then came the winter and Mother decided I had better have a job to earn a little money. So she was able to get me a job working at the chemist's in the High Street. My job was to develop films which had been brought in by various customers and I had to resort to a small outbuilding at the bottom of the back yard premises. I reached this room by a flight of wooden steps and a Mr Bishop was here in charge of all film processing. At first I felt very strange, and lonely too. There were no young people and the day seemed never to end. By the end of the first week I had decided I wouldn't like this job at all and was already feeling depressed, so I told Mr Jordan I would not be staying on. But on the Friday, my job was to weigh up a variety of powders and such like in the rear of the shop. Had this been the job I was to do I felt I would have liked it, there being more company too, but I still decided to find a job more to my liking.

At this time Brenner's Bazaar was just opening at the lower end of the High Street and several of my friends were already working there. The shop covered a large area towards the north end of the town adjoining a fresh fish shop (later to be 'Downtide' West's) and the telephone exchange (now Martella). So Mother made enquiries and I was told there was job if I liked to go and see the manageress, a Miss Howlett. Needless to say, this suited me down to the ground as there was also the probability that I would be with my friends. The shop sold all manner of things. I was in charge of the china counter. Everything was exceedingly cheap - 6d and 9d. It was lovely to unpack crates of china and glass and price it up for display purposes. Another counter sold haberdashery, others had soaps and sodas and household items, articles of clothing, babies' clothes, toys and games, sweets and chocolates. I often helped the manageress to dress the windows. Our boss, Mr Brenner, came occasionally to see all of us girls, greeting us with 'Good day to you.' He often brought several young lads from Norwich for a day's outing to the beach. Sadly he was killed in a road accident in Lincolnshire. The hours we worked were from 9 a.m. to 6 p.m. every day with half day on Wednesday. But on Saturday we all worked until 9 o'clock at night, having time off for lunch and also half an hour for our tea. For this I earned 15/- per week and gave my mother 10/-. After paying my stamp I was left with 4/2d with which to do everything.

The shop staff consisted of about eight assistants, the manageress and an errand boy, Eric Gant. He was sent off delivering goods to our customers and spent a great deal of his time in the large warehouse at the back of the shop sorting out all the goods received. He spent many hours out there; in the summer it wasn't too bad, but when the long, dark winter afternoons set in, with no heating and little illumination it could be quite lonely as much of it was dark and old. We told him it was haunted and he took us so seriously that it got almost impossible for him to stay there. Some of us would creep in and make low moaning noises. Poor Eric, he certainly had a lot to put up with from some of us girls, but all in all I think he probably enjoyed it as much as we did.

Of course, most of the shops kept open on a Saturday night, all lit up with gas lamps. The High Street would be very busy with the carts coming and going and the 'Midnight Milkman', as we called him, coming into town with his horse and cart.

I stayed working at Brenner's until 1936. Then, during the winter, my father fell and broke his ankle and I was needed at home and then, when summer came, I had to help with the visitors again.

Our amusements were limited; lack of money and of available social gatherings kept most of us indoors in the evenings. Quite a few of us joined the Junior Imperial League. This was a branch of a political party for the younger members of the family and did give us the chance of mixing with others of the same age group and the possibility of meeting members of the opposite sex. We were often at some of the larger houses in the town, either playing table tennis or darts or just drinking tea. Then, on other evenings, we were invited to Holt or Cromer to take part in a competition of some kind. This meant a bus ride or a lift by car.

Mother always attended all the political meetings and, when young, I had to accompany her. It was always very exciting when the winning candidate toured all the villages of North Norfolk after his victory. I well remember a very dark, stormy night when the heavens opened and rain bucketed down. The streets were lined with folk all waiting to see Lord Noel Buxton being towed into the town, a group of strong men pulling on the ropes each side of his car and cheering crowds excitedly urging them on despite the downpour.

Some of us who had little money to spare would attend the magic lantern show at the Salvation Army every now and again. This was often free, but the main enjoyment of those days was to go to the silent films in the Picture House on Cromer Road. Later this was to become a shoe factory with many girls employed here for a Norwich firm. It didn't cost us a lot to go to the films then. Often we paid one penny for a performance, sometimes threepence for the seats at the back. These were behind a velvet curtain which divided the better class seats, priced at ninepence, from the cheaper ones. Before we all went in we would buy bags of monkey nuts from a small grocer stall near by. By the time we came out the floor would be carpeted with crushed and broken shells. Halfway through the performance, some of us would attempt to creep up and seat ourselves in the 'posh' seats, but when the lights went up again, the superintendent, a Mr Catchpole (he had one hand only, the other a hook, a memento of the First World War) would storm down the aisles and march us all back again. Mr Walter Sadler had been the enterprising businessman who built the cinema. There was a smaller one near the Town Clock. We often called this the 'Flea House', but it had at first been the Town Hall where all the town's functions were held, such as fetes, pelting for the pig and grand occasions like Queen Victoria's Jubilee celebrations. Today it is the site of the very popular Little Theatre.

Our Saturday penny gave us great excitement when we went to see Charlie Chaplin, Buster Keaton and the famous Pearl White. We never knew what calamity was to befall her. She might be secured to a railway line with the fast approaching train bearing down on her, or hanging by her fingers to a crumbling cliff-top edge, to be interrupted by the magic words 'See Next Week's Episode'. We would emerge from the cinema, sure that our darling would be killed, only to go back next week and find that she was rescued, always in the nick of time. Accompanying all this excitement was a piano in the corner of the hall at which sat an ancient pianist tinkling the keys, either loud or soft music according to the drama of the film. One of the last films to be shown at this cinema was appropriately enough entitled 'Hallelujah' and ended the silents here. Just around the corner Mr Sadler had opened the Regent Hall, a very splendid building by all standards and this we all patronised. It was built in 1926 and housed the Sheringham Players and Operatic Society. Often my friend and I got a free ticket to their rehearsals as her step-sisters were in the cast. It was a rare treat for us actually to see and hear a live performance. This was very popular with all the visitors and the house was full every night. Some of the productions which I can remember were 'Geisha', 'Quaker Girl', 'Miss Hook of Holland', 'Country Girl' and several Gilbert and Sullivan operas.

Then came the Talkies - a great event. The first one, as I recall, was Janet Gaynor and Charles Farrell in 'Sunny Side Up'. We were enthralled by it all and somehow found the money to go along almost weekly.

In the early days, when Sheringham was just coming into fashion with the many holiday-makers who flocked to the coast, there was a new attraction for many to enjoy situated in Church Street between two shops and entered by a small arcade. This led to a small grassed area containing a simply-constructed stage painted green with light timber framework and covered by a canvas awning with just an earth floor and wooden-backed seats. Some of the elite sat on deck chairs. This popular entertainment commenced in 1919 and was called the Arcade Lawn, run by Leedham's Entertainers and used during the summer months by touring concert parties. They usually only stayed for one week, sometimes with only six to eight in the company, and they often had to take on many roles. Comedians, impressionists, singers, dancers and instrumentalists performed all sorts of romantic ballads, short sketches, dramas and domestic comedies. The concert party would stay in various houses for the summer or for the length of time they were here. My mother, one summer, had the pleasure of Mr Walter Williams and his wife who was a film star. He was one of the lead singers and often practised all day at our home, much to the annoyance of my father who had to be up early for his fishing and needed time in the day for rest.

The shows started at 8 p.m., after the many folks who stayed in the hotels had had their dinner. They would arrive in their evening gowns, parading in for all the locals to see, some of whom remarked on the strong smell of moth-balls as they swished by. Amongst the celebrities who first trod these boards were Clarkson Rose, Leslie Henson, Jack and Claude Hulbert and Cicely Courtnedge. From this world of the stage came Sir John Martin Harvey the actor and Ben Davies the Welsh tenor. The Box Office was to the left as one went in and there was an exit which led out of another small alley way. To add to the drama, when there was a downpour of rain, the roof let the rain in and the congregation often had to leave hurriedly.

By 1936 Weybourne Camp had come into existence as an anti-aircraft station involving territorial and regular soldiers. Most of my girl friends and myself had been strictly forbidden 'to talk to the soldiers' by our parents. If by chance we spoke to one or two wearing civilian dress and we found out by their conversation that they were from the camp, we quickly took to our heels and fled!

Our evenings were often spent walking the full length of the promenade and back, several times, occasionally speaking to the boys as they too were promenading. On

Monday evenings the Sheringham Temperance Silver Band, under Bandmaster Wallwork, would play for the enjoyment of large audiences, seated in deck chairs on the Tank Shelter area, East End promenade. Then again the same band would entertain all to an evening of music on the Leas every Thursday. Some folks would start dancing, but most would be enjoying the spectacle of the gentry and ladies who were taking their after-dinner stroll near the Grand Hotel, all in their evening dress and the gentlemen smoking huge cigars.

Beach scene c. 1931. Note the many tents on stones and promenade with coconut matting placed for easy access to the sands.

How different the beaches and promenades were in those far off days. Scores of tents lined both ends of the town with two if not three rows of tents and deck chairs on the beaches, especially along the East promenade and on the stones below. Now the sea encroaches all the time and tents would never be safe there at all. For the whole length of the promenade were canvas tents with visitors and holiday-makers all enjoying their vacation with tables and chairs, teapots and cups and saucers, picnic hampers. On the beaches, large groups were either playing cricket or tennis. From the promenade, besides the usual slopes which led down to the sand, were extra wooden ones placed for easier access. Also crossing each breakwater, again for the benefit of those on the beach, were large wide steps leading from one side of the beach to the other, so there was no problem of getting over as there is today. Large strips of fawny-brown coconut matting were rolled out and down the stones to the sand, making for more comfort. This was hauled up when the tide came in, stacked up on top of the stones ready for use again when needed. The beach inspectors, three or four worthy souls, walked along repeatedly and did a fine job of controlling any likely elements bent on doing damage. If one attempted to climb the slopes there was a stern warning of court cases and we did as we were told.

How clean the streets were! I don't remember seeing any litter blowing about and what a joy it was to us children when the Council cart came, especially on a boiling hot day, as it slowly went along spraying water everywhere, washing away the dirt and grime. We would follow behind with bare feet enjoying it all.

We would follow behind with bare feet.

Close to the Grand Hotel were rows of ponies and horses waiting to be hired out to youngsters for a few shillings. They did a gentle trot along to the War Memorial and back again. These were mostly owned by the Knowles family.

For some of the very youngest there was the Children's Special Service Mission. There was a continuous service provided for all those on holiday each day throughout the summer. There were beach sports and games and in the evening a procession of Chinese lanterns parading around the town.

The Daily Mail Sand Competition was again a highlight of the summer months. I remember being persuaded to enter for it by my mother and she gave me the slogan 'Daily Mail for King and Country'. I thought that was a good idea and went along to take part in the fun. I had planned to build a crown and a map of England, but just before I started, the little visitor girl who was staying at our house asked could she join me. I didn't have the courage to say no and of course, when I won the first prize of two pounds, I had to share it with her. I was a little bit saddened perhaps, but nevertheless the money was very handy. I was, I believe, about eleven years old. Old Mr William Hannah presented me with the prize and there were photos in the Daily Mail the next day.

Sometimes, if we were lucky, we would take our tennis racquets and go for a game of tennis on the Rec. This was a splendid sports area where football matches could be played, carnivals held and fireworks displays organised. It was a large area off the main road out of Sheringham going towards Upper Sheringham and was owned by Mr Upcher. He had encouraged the youth of Sheringham to participate in all kinds of sport by creating the Recreation Ground; football was its main sport and there were cricket pitches and several tennis courts with tournaments being held during July, August and September. On the Recreation Ground there was a green painted pavilion where all sorts of refreshments could be obtained and a grandstand for the supporters of the local football matches. We could use the tennis courts, if available, for a small fee during the mornings.

Whilst at school I was very pleased when library books were made available for us girls to borrow each week. After leaving school I was very envious of my sister and brother who could get books from the school library, but we had to be old enough to join. The County Library had started in the Sheringham Girls School, using one of the classrooms two evenings a week. At last I was old enough to join. Then the library was moved into the cookery class in George Street where large cupboards were filled with books, available for our own choosing. I found the reading of books and the borrowing of many hundreds of books relating to painting and sketching a sheer delight. It was a constant wonder that we could obtain all this valuable material for free.

About this time I went to work for hairdressers, Mr and Mrs G. Roe, who had a very good business in Station Road and remained with them until the outbreak of World War II.

Previous to this, in 1938, I had met the young man whom I was destined to marry. He was in the Royal Navy and the following years were to bring their ups and downs.